CHOICES

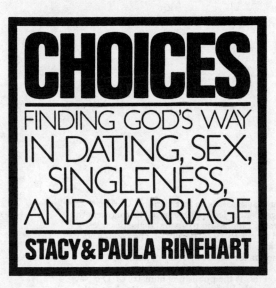

CHOICES

FINDING GOD'S WAY IN DATING, SEX, SINGLENESS, AND MARRIAGE

STACY & PAULA RINEHART

NAVPRESS

A MINISTRY OF THE NAVIGATORS
P.O. Box 6000, Colorado Springs, CO 80934

The Navigators is an international Christian
organization. Jesus Christ gave His followers the
Great Commission to go and make disciples
(Matthew 28:19). The aim of The Navigators is
to help fulfill that commission by multiplying
laborers for Christ in every nation.

NavPress is the publishing ministry of The Navigators. NavPress publications are tools to help
Christians grow. Although publications alone cannot make disciples or change lives, they can help
believers learn biblical discipleship and apply
what they learn to their lives and ministries.

© 1982 by Stacy and Paula Rinehart
All rights reserved, including translation
Library of Congress Catalog Card Number:
  82-062701
ISBN: 0-89109-494-6
14944

Seventh printing, 1986

Unless otherwise identified, all Scripture quota-
tions are from the *Holy Bible: New International
Version* (NIV). Copyright © 1973, 1978, 1984,
International Bible Society. Used by permission
of Zondervan Bible Publishers. Other versions
quoted are the *King James Version* (KJV).; *The Living Bible* (LB), © 1971 by Tyndale House Publishers, used by permission; and the *New American
Standard Bible* (NASB), © The Lockman Foundation 1960, 1962, 1963, 1968, 1971, 1972, 1973,
1975, 1977.

Printed in the United States of America

Contents

To
Gordon and Brenda Van Amburgh
and
John and Karen D'Arrezzo

whose help and influence
guided the choices we made
concerning dating, courtship, and marriage.

Authors

Stacy Rinehart holds a D.Min. from Trinity Evangelical Divinity School. He is the director of the Leadership Development Institute at Glen Eyrie in Colorado Springs, Colorado. Previously, he served as the Navigator representative in Tulsa, Oklahoma, coordinating ministries in northeast Oklahoma. He also directed the Navigator student ministry at Oklahoma State University. Stacy came into contact with The Navigators at Fort Benning, Georgia, while serving as an officer in the U.S. Army.

Paula Corn Rinehart is a graduate of the University of Tennessee, where she was involved with The Navigators.

In addition to *Choices*, the Rineharts have written *Living in Light of Eternity* (NavPress, 1986).

Stacy and Paula live in Colorado Springs with their two children, Allison and Brady.

Foreword

Robert Flack writes in *Better Than Gold*, "Getting married is easy. Staying married is more difficult. Staying happily married for a lifetime should rank among the fine arts."

How true! But many of the choices related to a happy marriage are made years before two people say "I do." And often the foundation critical to a lifetime of wedded happiness is cracked or eroded by wrong choices during those years. Without a great deal of thought as Christians, we buy what the world is selling. In our dating relationships we fail to search for God's principles. Then we hope he will wave a magic wand on our wedding day and erase from our minds the tapes by which our relationships have been programmed for so long. That isn't going to happen!

To help you make the right choices from now on, Stacy and Paula Rinehart have researched and written a book that is biblically based and spiritually sound, giving principles which, if followed, will help build a strong structure for a lasting and successful marriage.

You may not agree with all the Rineharts present, but you will be challenged to think through—to pray through—the ideas and then to form your convictions.

May you not drift through your dating relationships, but may you determine your convictions and then, with God's help, live by them. A principle worth carving deep into every day is, "In all your ways acknowledge him, and he will make your paths straight" (Proverbs 3:6).

Jack Mayhall

Preface

Paula, I give you this ring as a token of my love for you. God has built into you the qualities essential to become my wife. You've added joy, creativity, and beauty to my life. I promise to love you, constantly giving up my rights for you even as Christ did for his bride, the Church. I promise to lead you as God directs in our lives and to be responsible for your well-being and the well-being of our children. I always want you to be my best friend. Regardless of what happens in our lives, we can rejoice and enjoy life because God has enclosed us in his hand. We love, Paula, because God first loved us.

Stacy, because I have seen God lead us together in such a special way, I give myself to making our marriage and our life such that the world looking on will know that he is real. I promise that I will love you in the midst of the everydayness of life. I promise that I will live openly and honestly before you so that we would not live out our lives in separation and isolation. Because I trust you with my life, I promise that I will defer to your leadership. Before God and before men, you will be the head of our home. And so do not urge me to leave you or to turn back from following you. For where you go, I will go; where you lodge, I will lodge. Your people will be my people and your God, my God. And thus may the Lord do to me and worse, if anything but death should part you and me.

We began life together on August 4, 1973 with these words. To leave the impression that it was all as simple as repeating pleasant phrases, though, would be deceiving. The struggles we encountered and the choices we made for years prior to that soft, white day in August are what this book is about.

Our enemy, being the author of lies, beckons us to choose to walk the broad path of the world, promising more freedom and pleasure with every step. In truth, those who follow such a path find that what they thought would be satisfaction and pleasure become destruction and misery in the end.

God, however, asks us to enter by the narrow gate, which, though it seems restrictive, nevertheless leads to life. God is no man's debtor, and those who discipline themselves to obey him find the freedom and fulfillment they so desired.

It is our hope that those who read this book will be motivated, in this area of dating, relating, and choosing a mate, to choose to enter by the narrow gate and experience the life God promises.

Stacy and Paula Rinehart

Acknowledgements

This book could not have been written without the encouragement and help of many people. The critique and input of various Navigator staff, especially Jack and Carolyn Hill, and Mike and Judie Crouse, have been invaluable to us. We appreciate those who served us ably in field testing the study material with students at Oklahoma State University. We also wish to thank Denise Bower for the hours she labored in typing the manuscript. And last, but not least, we thank Jean Stephens for the careful, thorough job she did in editing this book.

How to Get the Most Out of This Book

What one is told, one soon forgets. What one discovers for himself is not soon forgotten.

We urge you to answer the questions in the Dating Knowledge Inventory before you read this book. As you read each chapter, you will see our convictions—but they may not be yours. When you study the questions at the end of each chapter, you will develop your own convictions from first-hand exposure to the Scriptures.

Dating Knowledge Inventory

1. How would you define a date?

2. Do you think it is permissible for a Christian to

date a non-Christian? Explain your answer.

3. List as many passages as you can about sexual purity.

4. Give the references for the two most important passages in Scripture on the subject of marriage. List two other important passages.

5. How many times have you studied each passage? (Reading a passage does not mean you studied it.)

6. Using Scripture, have you studied the role of a wife and the role of a husband?

7. Is marriage to a non-Christian an option for a Christian? Give references to support your answer.

8. What qualities do you want in a mate? What Scripture is your list based on?

9. Have you studied singleness in the Scriptures? What are the key passages?

10. Describe your attitude toward dating, singleness, and marriage.

1

Going Against the Grain of Your Culture

IMAGINE YOURSELF in a new restaurant reading a fancy menu on an empty stomach. You spend a few minutes deciphering the delicacies listed and then give your order. "I believe I'll try this roast duckling with chestnut sauce, please." When the plate arrives, you express your approval of a beautiful arrangement of food, complete with complementary colors and garnishes. "It's worth blowing a diet for food like this," you remark.

About halfway through the meal, you begin to have second thoughts. The chestnuts are lodging in your throat. It seems like that duck and your stomach are fighting over mineral rights. "Maybe my eyes are bigger than my stomach," you explain with a note of regret as you push back your plate. Mentally you resolve to ask a few questions and make a wise decision the next time you look at an unfamiliar menu.

Many people go through similar pangs of regret concerning their decisions about dating, courtship, and marriage. Relationships that are appealing at the outset can turn distasteful with time. The gentle wound of Cupid's arrow can become a painful thorn in the flesh, and many who swear by their commitment to each other soon find that they are swearing at it. In fact, the statistics show that typically you will have no more than a fifty-fifty chance for a lasting and happy marital union. As one counselor said, "There are many people living heaven on earth and they call it marriage and many people living hell on earth and they call it marriage. You can only rejoice with people who have discovered a partner and have been able to work out a relationship under divine principles and with divine enabling that can only adequately be described as heaven on earth. And you can only bleed for those people who for a variety of reasons are in a situation where they are living in a daily, constant hell."[1] What a comfort that in Christ you don't have to be statistically "typical."

Anyone familiar with current divorce statistics would agree that our culture is doing a poor job of preparing people for lasting and fulfilling marriages. Could it be that problems lie in the nature of the dating and courting relationships that precede the marriage vows? I think so.

Stacy and I have observed that although most single Christians really want to experience the uniqueness of a Christian home, they're unaware of the non-Christian pressures of our culture that greatly weaken that desire. All too often, before they've developed spiritual discernment, their ships are blown off course by prevailing cultural winds.

Dating relationships as we know them are relatively new on the scene. They have no direct precedent in the Scriptures. (The only Hebrew matchmakers were the parents of the prospective bride and groom!)

What does emerge from Scripture, however, are relationship principles that are clear, trans-cultural, and timeless. For instance, the Bible teaches, "Abstain from sinful desires, which war against your soul" (1 Peter 2:11). In Corinth many centuries ago, the application of that verse might have been "Stay away from the temple prostitutes." In our culture today it might mean, "Check the rating on a movie before you decide to see it."

Yet while the Bible speaks quietly in timeless principles, our culture shouts its message in dictums difficult to ignore. And we are shaped by a message we aren't even aware that we're hearing. How can that be? In simple terms, our culture is our background. It all seems so right, so normal because these influences have become a part of us. Our cultural background is a "switch" that is difficult to turn off as we acquire our outlook on life.

My Experience

I have experienced both kinds of relationships—that which is typical of our generation's mentality concerning dating, and one built on the firm foundation of God's principles. There is little in common and a great deal of contrast between the two.

My first love was a guy I'll call Sam, and his first love was basketball. Sam had been a Christian from childhood and yet never elevated his hunger for God above the thrill of placing that brown ball through a hoop. In the process of our dating, though, he and his family were responsible for my conversion. Beyond that, only two things were right about our relationship; we were both Christians, and he was a guy and I was a girl.

We were regulars at church, of course, and even occasionally discussed the sermons. But our relationship was based on the cornerstone of physical attraction, and we were each a security blanket for the other. We went through five years of the typical ups and downs marked by jealousy and selfishness. Had we not been so emotionally involved, we would have broken up much sooner. As it was, our parting late in our college years was painfully close to a miniature divorce.

We both knew for months that our relationship was not what it ought to be. We were miserable with each other and just as miserable without each other. Getting out of the car and closing the door on that relationship ended a chapter of my life. I had known Sam for so long that facing the reality of no future relationship with him was like adjusting to a divorce or his death.

I forced myself to turn my focus from Sam and place my total dependence on the Lord. And God stepped into the emptiness in my life and began to meet the needs for which I had unsuccessfully looked to Sam. I found out just how much I'd been missing! By the time God brought Stacy into my life, I had learned something of what it meant to depend on the Lord alone and to enjoy his sufficiency.

I was no longer searching for a new relationship, but what would you do if you found yourself in a car pool forty minutes a day with a guy? You'd try to make normal conversation. But after about two weeks I decided that either I was very boring, or Stacy was a recluse!

One day, though, I mentioned racquetball, and he began to talk nonstop. I was so amazed that when he began to ask questions about the length of my racquet and how many sides to the court I preferred, I completely made up my answers. I had never seen a racquetball in my life! As soon as I got out of the car, I was stabbed with the realization that I had actually lied and would be faced with the humble admission of truth the next day. Somehow, though, that confession broke the ice, and we spent a delightful summer getting to know each other in our daily forty-minute car pool.

From that point on, we spent hours talking together in person and then over long distance via cassette tapes. Because our relationship was marked by the lack of physical involvement (not lack of physical attraction), we really got to know each other's goals, dreams, and backgrounds. In fact, I felt I knew Stacy better than I had ever known any other guy before—Christian or non-Christian—because I knew more of his total personality. My overwhelming emotion at that point was one of *respect* which eventually melted into genuine love.

The world knows little of this kind of love—the variety that says, "I know you well—your strengths and your faults—and I accept you anyway." When we married a year later, we were both convinced that God had led us together and that our relationship was "the Lord's doing, and marvelous in our eyes." Engraved inside our wedding bands is this verse—"We love because he first loved us" (1 John 4:19).

Sad to say, my relationship with Sam represented a typical dating relationship for many people. For Christians, that doesn't have to be the case. But our culture exerts such a strong pull on our lives that we can easily be brainwashed into following the patterns around us.

The Ways of the Nations

As we mature in the Christian life, we begin to objectively reevaluate the kaleidoscope of influences in our background. Our approach to the dating process is especially crucial. Our culture exerts such a strong pull on our lives that we can easily become brainwashed into following the patterns around us, only to arrive on the other side of the altar with a "ho-hum" marriage. God warns us, "Do not learn the ways of the nations. . . . For the customs of the peoples are worthless" (Jeremiah 10:2-3). What are some of these ways?

Living for the Moment
Our three-year-old daughter is having trouble learning her last name, Rinehart. If you asked Allison her name, you'd be surprised to hear her say "Allison Right Now!" Actually it's no wonder she thinks that's her last name because her daily chatter contains a barrage of "right now."

As adults we are no different except to call the demand for the immediate "instant gratification," a phrase that accurately describes our generation. This determination to have what we want right now is like approaching life with a vending machine mentality. Just look over the possibilities, decide what you want, and get it immediately.

The philosophy of living for the moment is everywhere. "You only go around once in life, so grab for all the gusto you can get." "If it feels good, do it." "If you're angry, explode and you'll feel better." James said, "You lust and do not have; so you commit murder" (James 4:2, NASB), meaning that you fulfill your passions immediately, even if you have to sacrifice another person's welfare.

John and Pat were two young Christians who had known each other only a short time before they came to us for premarital counseling. It quickly became evident that they were immature emotionally and spiritually and their relationship was based on a physical attraction. They desperately needed to wait and give themselves time.

They had taken a bite of the "right-now" apple, however, and we could not dissuade them from the wedding scheduled within the week. They found after marriage that when their initial attraction to each other wore off, they had married someone they didn't really know. Five difficult years of financial woes, small children, and marital counseling have demonstrated to them the repercussions of living for the pleasure of the moment. As we have watched and counseled them in some of the difficulties of these years, how often we've wished we had more adamantly opposed that wedding.

This couple is a clear illustration of why some pastors refuse to marry two people who have not been seriously courting for at least six months. It simply takes time to really know someone. If John and Pat had known each other longer without the complication of physical involvement, they might have avoided a disappointing marriage.

Living for the moment not only affects decisions to get married, but also attitudes toward marriage after it takes place. As indicated by the sign in a shop that states, "We rent wedding rings, " marriage has become a contract for "as long as our love lasts" rather than a commitment of lifelong permanence.

A friend got married the same summer Stacy and I did, and I well remember a startling conversation with her. I asked what she and Don thought about when to have children. She replied, "Oh, we're definitely going to wait and see if our relationship works out. We'd hate to bring children into a broken marriage." Marriage for keeps was a maybe-or-maybe-not proposition in her mind.

For Christians, that mentality is unthinkable because Scripture teaches that marriage is the symbolic picture of Christ's union with his bride, the church (Ephesians 5:23). In spite of our unfaithfulness as the bride, he is committed to us for all eternity. Based on that relationship, divorce is not an option for two believers; to entertain the possibility means you shouldn't be thinking of marriage. To a culture that lives for the moment and marries for the moment, the Christian's concept of lifelong commitment to one person stands out in sharp contrast.

Scripture uses a vocabulary quite different from our generation and culture. In the Bible we see synonyms for words like *discipline, restraint, waiting, responsibility,* and *commitment,* to name only a few. Though it might sometimes appear that God would like to thwart all of our fun, nothing could be further from the truth. "For I know the plans I have for you. . . . They are plans for good and not for evil, to give you a future and a hope" (Jeremiah 29:11, *The Living Bible*).

When I was a young but growing Christian, God began speaking to me about habits in my dating life that were hindering my spiritual growth. The most notable was that of dating non-Christian guys. But I put plugs in my ears for this reason: listening to God on that issue would uproot my entire lifestyle. I knew very few Christians then, and the ones I knew didn't go out very often. The price of not dating unbelievers could well be spending many nights alone as I watched my friends go out.

However, God gradually got my attention through his word. As I began to trust him with smaller issues and saw his faithfulness, I found courage to believe that following his principles in dating would not leave me shortchanged. First Peter 2:6 (NASB) was the verse I claimed again and again: "He who believes in him shall not be disappointed."

I realized that to take the easiest route, to live for the momentary enjoyment of going out more often with non-Christians, could cost me the quality relationship God might have for me in the future. I believed that if I trusted and obeyed God in this area, I would not be disappointed in the future marriage God might have for me.

God does not place an emphasis on the *now*. You, God's unique creation, are in the process of *becoming* all that he intended you to be when he paid the price to free you from sin's power. And he is ever so capable of bringing the right person into your life—on his timetable, not yours. When it comes to dating, courtship, and marriage, the stakes are simply too high to live for the moment.

Living for the Sensual
Possibly no phenomenon has had quite as much bearing on the cultural mores of dating as has the sexual revolution

of this century. Bookstore shelves are overloaded with manuals on developing better techniques. Supposedly, any activity is permissible now for those in love. Sexual experimentation before marriage is applauded as a viable means of determining compatibility and acquiring skills. License is the order of the day. What does this permissiveness add up to? Chuck Swindoll quotes an excellent article by Richard Cohen, originally appearing in the *Washington Post*. It was entitled, "Open Marriage . . . Broken Marriage."

> There were these couples I know. They were open. They were honest. They were having affairs. They were not sneaking around (applause), they were not lying (applause), they were being honest (whistles). They were being open. Everyone agreed that it was wonderful. The men agreed and the women agreed and I agreed and it all made you wonder. Then they split. There was something wrong. Invariably someone couldn't take it. It had nothing to do with the head. The head understood. It was the heart; it was, you should pardon the expression, broken.
>
> It all made you think. It made you think that maybe there are things we still don't know about men and women and maybe before we spit in the eye of tradition we ought to know what we're doing. I have some theories and one of them is that one of the ways you measure love is not with words, but with actions, with commitment, with what you are willing to give up, with what you are willing to share with no one else.[2]

If we could take the input of our culture in the area of sex, turn it upside down and inside out and discard some of it entirely, we might begin to approach the instructions that God gave in the first place. Just as a car manual gives detailed information as to the use and abuse of your car, so God has given us explicit directives as to the use and abuse of sex. As its Creator, he designed the physical expression of love for the context of permanence and commitment found only in marriage.

Consider the irony of it all. The same God who spoke the world into existence also masterminded our physical relationships, and yet the world acts as if he were some prudish old maid ready to give us a slap on the wrist for holding hands. God declared that all he had made was "very good" (Genesis 1:31). He devoted one book in the Bible, Song of Songs (Song of Solomon), primarily to a description of the heights of physical enjoyment possible in married love.

The world has a shortsighted, painfully inadequate understanding of all that God meant sex to be. Sex involves all that you are as a person brought together with another whole person to reflect the complete oneness of Christ and his bride, the church. And just as Richard Cohen said, sex is special precisely because it's shared with only one person.

Living for Someone Who Loves You
"You're Nobody Til Somebody Loves You" is a familiar song. For much of our adolescent years and then some, we're subtly led to believe that when we find that special someone, our lives will take on real meaning. Our personalities will blossom, and our imperfections will disappear.

Many people wake up in married life to realize that what once seemed like moonlight and roses is now daylight and dishes. They are the same people with the same fears, old habits, and insecurities that they had before they married. And they are each married to someone who will help point out these inconsistencies! Finding that special someone is not the ultimate answer to a person's needs.

However, there is some truth to the assertion that happiness is having someone to love you. It's just that the world has the wrong someone in mind! No human relationship can fill that God-shaped vacuum that lies inside us all. As Augustine said, "We were made for God Himself and our hearts are restless until they find their rest in Thee." David reminds us that "in Thy presence is fullness of joy; in Thy right hand, there are pleasures forever" (Psalm 16:11, NASB).

In spite of this right relationship with God, have you ever felt even mild panic at the realization that there is no one person particularly interested in you, or maybe no one who arouses your interest? That can be a rather hollow sense of aloneness sometimes. At that pivotal point you can be deluded by our culture into a quiet but frantic search for that special someone. You can even begin to feel angry with God and somehow cheated because he doesn't understand and meet your need, failing to remember that only he can satisfy the bottomless craving of your heart.

Until we acknowledge that we are made first and foremost for God and that in Christ we have been made complete (Colossians 2:10), we will quite naturally fall into the world's trap of seeking our fulfillment in a relationship with another person. And a relationship built on that basis will leave us disappointed as we see that person fail. We're all sinners, redeemed and unredeemed. We must become rightly related to God (the vertical dimension) in order for our relationship with another person (the horizontal dimension) to take on real meaning.

The world prods us along in a futile search to find ultimate fulfillment in another person, but because it cannot be found, most people remain quite unfulfilled. That deprivation causes them to continue trying to *get* from a relationship. They unconsciously ask the question, How can you meet my needs? As the author of Proverbs wrote, "There is a way that seems right to a man, but in the end it leads to death" (Proverbs 14:12). By way of contrast, a Christian truly fulfilled in Christ is able to *give* in a relationship because his most basic needs have already been met by his relationship to God. In his love and his timing God brings into a union two people who are looking to him for their ultimate fulfillment. And two people who are seeking to give, not get, spell out a good marriage in large letters.

Considering the sacrificial love of God for his children, it must cause him both anger and pain when we make an idol of a human relationship. Anytime we allow a person to be foremost in our thoughts and to be the goal of our existence, we're heading for disaster. Elaine Stedman writes in a poem, "Only he deserves to be our first love."

The Choice Is Yours

You cannot just stumble along the path of what seems natural and appealing to you at the moment without encountering consequences at some point. "Be happy, young man, while you are young, and let your heart give you joy in the days of your youth. Follow the ways of your heart and whatever your eyes see, but know that for all these things God will bring you to judgment" (Ecclesiastes 11:9).

When you consider the powerful influence of our culture from our impressionable years on—pressuring us to live for the moment, to live for the sensual, and to live for ourselves—it's a wonder that we can escape without harm. Clearly our only hope is to be transformed by the renewing of our minds (Romans 12:2), and this metamorphosis takes place through consistent intake of the word.

To make the right choices in the area of dating is indeed a battle, because the pressures are so great. God's most powerful weapon for insured victory is his word. The more alive the Scriptures are to you personally, the more your thinking will change and your behavior will follow.

When Stacy and I were first married, I had the same dream several times. I would be floating through a fog down the aisle of a church to marry a man whose face was sometimes indistinguishable and sometimes that of a former boyfriend. Always the same sick feeling in my stomach cautioned me that I was making a mistake. As I reached the end of the aisle, I would awaken in a cold sweat and then be flooded with relief that the person next to me was Stacy and that I had made no mistake. I would lie there and profusely praise God for saving me from that mistake.

Only after marriage could I fully appreciate the significance of my earlier choices. Sometimes they were only small choices; often they were quite painful. Whether easy or difficult, those choices actually determined the future course of my life.

The illusion of youth is, "I have all my life before me. My choices right now won't make any difference." Yet in the span of a few short but crucial years, decisions are made that open or close some doors for a lifetime. All of a sudden it's too late to develop solid friendships with the opposite sex, or exercise more sexual restraint, or study harder and party less. Life has moved on.

Going against the grain of your culture means a willingness to reject a sensual, self-centered lifestyle. The choices entailed are not often very simple and almost always require some backbone. Anytime you yield an area of your life previously under the world's influence to the Lordship of Christ, you encounter a struggle. In her book *Out of the Saltshaker*, Rebecca Pippert writes, "Christianity isn't a narcotic that dulls you into obedience. It involves battle—it's excruciating to give up control. . . . Heaven will not be filled with innocent people, running around saying, 'Oh, was there another way? I guess I never noticed.'"[3]

Moses spoke some timely words that apply to these choices set before you at this point in your life. "See, I am setting before you today a blessing and a curse—the blessing if you obey the commands of the Lord your God that I am giving you today; the curse if you disobey the commands of the Lord your God" (Deuteronomy 11:26-28).

God in his sovereignty has left you the guidance of his word and the prompting of the Holy Spirit. But ultimately your will is free; and the choice is yours.

Notes   1. Stuart Briscoe, from the tape "A Call to Singleness."

2. Richard Cohen, "Open Marriage . . . Broken Marriage," *The Washington Post*, as quoted by Charles R. Swindoll in *Strike the Original Match* (Multnomah Press, 1980), pages 36-37.

3. Rebecca Pippert, *Out of the Saltshaker* (InterVarsity Press, 1979), page 64.

Questions for Personal Study and Application

1. List the sources that have most influenced your dating patterns.

2. Describe a dating relationship in your past. How did culture influence this relationship? How did Scripture influence this relationship?

3. Read Genesis 25:29-34.
   a. How did Esau live for the moment, and what were the consequences?
   b. In what ways do you see Esau's attitude reflected in your decision making?

4. Read 2 Samuel 11:1-12:15.
   a. How did David live for the sensual?
   b. What were the consequences of his sin?

5. In what way, if any, have you been living for the sensual? What will you do to change this?

6. Read Genesis 39.
   a. What are some character qualities that prevented Joseph from taking advantage of his regular opportunity for sin with Potiphar's wife?
   b. What are some principles from Joseph's life that can be applied to dating?

7. Define idolatry in your own words. According to God's word in 1 Corinthians 5:11 and 10:14, and Ephesians 5:5, what is his perspective on idolatry in our lives?

8. Read Romans 12:1-2.
   a. What does it mean to "present your bodies as a living and holy sacrifice, acceptable to God"?
   b. Have you ever presented yourself as a living sacrifice to God? What about your dating life?

9. Jot down one or two significant applications that you will make from this study.

Scripture memory assignment: Romans 12:1

Special project: Ask two or three Christian friends if they have committed their dating life to the Lord. If so, what difference does it make?

Questions for Discussion

Each group of questions below is for your use in discussing the corresponding questions on page 16. Notice that there are no discussion questions for questions five and nine. You may want to ask some of your own questions.

Question 1: What do you think are some of the reasons why the divorce rate is so high in our culture? In what way do you think modern dating practices have a bearing on the high divorce rate?

Question 2: The authors maintain that the culture determines our concept of dating. Do you agree? Why?

Question 3: If you had been present when Jacob and Esau had this encounter, what would you have encouraged Esau to do, and why?

Question 4: If you were a counselor of King David, what would you have counseled him when he first saw Bathsheba?

Question 6: Scan the section on "Living for the Moment." In what ways do you feel this temptation? How does this philosophy affect your life?

Read James 4:1-4. What are the results of living for pleasures and lusts (sensuality) listed in verses one and two? A pleasure-centered life is worldly. What are the results of being a friend of the world?

Question 7: In what ways can a dating relationship become an idol? How can you tell if that is happening to you?

Question 8: If a person has presented himself as a living sacrifice, what differences would it make in his dating life?

2
Priceless Principles

EVEN IF YOU never marry, dating is a socialization process that can contribute significantly to making you a well-rounded person. It should not be thought of only as a tool to acquire a mate. In most cases, however, the habits formed, attitudes acquired, and choices made during your dating years will have a direct bearing upon the quality and success of your relationship if you marry. In fact, many of the experiences of your dating life are useful and necessary preparation for marriage.

It's also true that your concept of what marriage could and should be helps determine the course you choose in dating. Motivation for reshaping aspects of your dating life often springs from a clearer picture of marriage the way God has laid it out, with all its potential, and his estimate of its importance.

Timeless Truths from a Garden Wedding

If you want to view the state of the art of any item on the market today—whether computers, cameras, or microwave ovens—you search for the latest model. In the realm of human technology, the most recent design is the best.

Not so with God. His original designs, whether they be a daisy, a baby, or a snowflake, are faultlessly perfect. Before there were parliaments and congresses, commerce and conglomerates, books, music, art, or systematic theology, God fashioned a woman from Adam's side, brought her to him, and declared openly his enormous pleasure as Matchmaker.

Turn with us to Genesis 2:18–23 for a look at the beginning of the most special of all human relationships—man and woman.

> The Lord God said, "It is not good for the man to be alone. I will make a helper suitable for him. . . .
>
> So the Lord God caused the man to fall into a deep sleep; and while he was sleeping, he took one of the man's ribs and closed up the place with flesh. Then the Lord God made a woman from the rib he had taken out of the man, and he brought her to the man.
>
> The man said,
> "This is now bone of my bones
>   and flesh of my flesh;
> she shall be called 'woman,'
>   for she was taken out of man."

First Things First

Adam first met his *Master*; his relationship with his Creator was firmly founded. Then God gave him his *mission* in life, that of tending the garden. Only then did God bring to Adam his *mate*. Not many people have reversed that sequence without experiencing undesirable consequences. Knowing God and knowing something of *what* you want to accomplish in life are as important as knowing *whom* you want to accomplish it with.

God's Provision for Adam's Needs

In this, the first of many marriages, God took the total responsibility for providing the suitable bride. Adam had only to cooperate with God's plan, so we find him asleep. Now, as then, the person who desires a "marriage made in heaven" waits for God's perfect timing and occupies himself with God's will for the present.

In this case, God's response to man's lonely existence was to provide a woman, or as the text says, "a helper." (Marriage is not always God's answer to loneliness.) Since the word *helper* is often used in Scripture to refer to God himself, the meaning is not degrading. "It conveys the idea of someone who 'assists another to reach complete fulfillment,'" says author Chuck Swindoll. "It is a beautiful picture of a dignified, necessary role filled by one whom God would make and bring alongside the man."[1]

Adam traded a rib for a wife. That was a profitable trade, wouldn't you say? Certainly we see no evidence of regret as Adam exclaimed, "This is it!" (*The Living Bible*). Adam recognized this woman to be exactly what he needed. Such a perfect creation as Eve revealed not only God's goodness but his intimate knowledge of Adam.

Four Principles
Genesis 2:24-25 is not only God's commentary on the union of Adam and Eve, but also provides truths basic to any marriage. In his book *Strike the Original Match*, Chuck Swindoll suggests that from these verses come four inviolable marriage principles.[2]

... a man shall leave his
    father and mother   SEVERANCE
... and shall cleave to his wife   PERMANENCE
... and they shall become one flesh UNITY
... and the man and his wife were
    both naked and were not ashamed INTIMACY

God doesn't offer any alternative lifestyles in marriage. His intention in bringing a man and woman together is that they establish a new family that is not merely an extension of their parental homes. They are to be bound together spiritually, psychologically, emotionally, and physically as long as they live.

Perhaps you could parallel these principles to the process of coming to Christ. When we become his children through faith in the finished work of the cross, we in effect sever our ties with the world and cleave to him. We grow in that unity and spiritual intimacy all the rest of our lives, until at long last, we dine with him at the marriage feast of the Lamb (see Revelation 19:7-9).

God's Seal of Approval

"Marriage should be honored by all" (Hebrews 13:4). Such were God's instructions through Paul. Marriage is not preferable to the single life, nor is it a higher calling; in either state, we serve God *first* and trust him to meet our needs. But marriage is a special relationship as indicated through Scripture: The first institution was marriage; Christ's first miracle occurred at a wedding; the New Testament includes many instructions concerning the marriage relationship; and in eternity we will celebrate the marriage feast of the Lamb.

Marriage in Christ is a privilege denied to angels and given only to men and women. Peter uses a beautiful phrase to describe it: "joint heirs of the grace of life" (1 Peter 3:7). God takes the relationship so seriously that he warns husbands (in the same verse) that insensitive treatment of their wives may render their prayers ineffective. Likewise, wives are reminded that living in conflict with their husbands and rejecting their leadership bring dishonor to God's word (Titus 2:5). God's plan is that when others look into a Christian home, the marriage in it will be an undeniable example of a faith that works.

Marriage is the first holy relationship God ordained. Our human concept of holiness is that which is enshrined, or set apart as untouchable. God, however, takes eternal truths, for which we use the word *holy*, and places them in the living relationships of his people. The lifelong union of a man and a woman is *holy* because it symbolizes in human form the unseverable love of Christ for his bride, the church. To tamper with the relationship is to meddle with one of God's original designs.

God is the beginning and the end of the relationship, that which holds it together. His love provides the pillar of support that enables a marriage to thrive while surrounded by the storms of life.

Worth Any Price

God is far more concerned about your life partner than you could ever be. Knowing that, why is this area of dating, courtship, and marriage such a lordship struggle for most Christians?

We believe that Satan wages incredibly active warfare in this tender matter of the heart. Compromise is his strategy, and a godly union is what he seeks to prevent.

A contemporary of Billy Graham came up to him years after they had both attended a conference. She asked, "Do you remember the night the missionary spoke? I committed my life to go to China, but I married a man with a different outlook. I've never gone anywhere and life is hell on earth." It was not the fear of difficult living conditions that compromised her commitment, but the choice of the wrong man.

George Sweeting, the president of Moody Bible Institute, gives a fascinating talk in which he traces the lineage in both his family and his wife's family back through three and four generations of godly, committed Christians. Many of us cannot claim such a spiritual heritage. Nevertheless, we can be the beginning of many generations to come, handing on to our children and their children the light of truth entrusted to us. Your choice in marriage influences not only the remainder of your life, but generations to come. The Lord desires godly seed from your union.

An older man and woman who had experienced a quarter of a century of marriage in the Lord once said to me, "We've found that when a couple united in heart and prayer comes before God, there is nothing in his will that he'll withhold. It seems to tap the power of God in a special way."

To be married to a man or woman who loves the Lord and wants to serve him is one of life's highest privileges. It's worth whatever the wait, whatever the cost.

Notes   1. Charles R. Swindoll, *Strike the Original Match* (Multnomah Press, 1980), page 19.

2. Swindoll, page 21.

Questions for Personal Study and Application

1. How would you define marriage?
2. Read Genesis 2:18–25.
   a. Why was woman created?
   b. Based on this passage, what is the marriage relationship to be like?
3. Read Ephesians 5:22–23.
   a. What is the responsibility of the wife to her husband?
   b. What does it mean for the wife to subject herself to her husband?
   c. Why is the wife to subject herself to her husband?
   d. What are the responsibilities of the husband to his wife?
   e. What does the term "*husbands love your wives*" mean today?
   f. Why is the husband to love his wife?
4. What are some things you want to be true of your marriage, should the Lord grant you that gift?
5. What are some things you want to be true of your future mate? Commit these to the Lord in prayer.
6. What needs do you have that a spouse could minister to? What needs could you meet for a spouse?
7. What new commitments affecting dating and marriage will you make as a result of this study?
8. Write down any unanswered questions you may have on the marriage relationship.

Scripture memory assignment: Ephesians 5:33

Special project: Ask two or three Christian friends what elements they think make a good marriage.

Questions for Discussion

Question 1: What major influences have had an effect on your concept of marriage?

Question 2: Why is our culture so opposed to the biblical design for marriage? How would you paraphrase verses twenty-four and twenty-five?

Question 3: How would you describe an ideal (biblical) relationship of a couple to their parents?

Read Ephesians 5:18-21. What context is established there for verses twenty-two through thirty-three? What are the characteristics of a spirit-filled life?

Question 7: What new thoughts about marriage came to you from the Genesis 2 and Ephesians 5 passages?

3

Healthy Dating
Relationships

FOR OUR PURPOSE in this book, we would like to define dating as any appointment between members of the opposite sex. That's a broad definition, but sometimes we associate dating only with dressing up, going somewhere special, and spending a lot of money. You can have a date throwing a frisbee!

Notice that we're not narrowing the concept of dating to one guy who takes out one girl. Going out together as a group has some decided advantages. The responsibility for entertaining a girl is gone, and with it, much of the pressure of evaluation. In a group situation, you can get to know someone and discern his or her commitment to the Lord at an uninvolved distance. Some people advocate going out in odd numbers such as three, five, or seven because it reduces the possibility of pairing off and lessens the temptation toward physical involvement. In short, going out as a group can provide you with a wealth of relationships and many evenings of just plain fun.

When a person is making the transition from a lifestyle of worldly, sensual dating relationships to a godly frame of reference, going out in groups can be the best way to meet his or her social needs. It's a time to step out of the classic dating mold altogether and give God an opportunity to revolutionize a person's perspective on guy / girl relationships. Then having come to his new convictions through studying God's word, he can resume one-to-one dating.

There should be some distinctive differences about your dating relationships as a Christian that an unbeliever could only attribute to the reality of Christ. The world will judge our Christianity by the love exhibited among us, including in our dating relationships. "All men will know that you are my disciples if you love one another" (John 13:35).

In a dating situation, this love manifests itself in the selfless characteristics of true biblical fellowship. It includes love without lust, honesty without cruelty, transparency without thoughtlessness, and relaxed conversation without self-centeredness. When these distinctives are visible, healthy dating relationships are a living example of Christianity for an onlooking world.

What does a healthy dating relationship look like? Recently a friend and I sat in a coffee shop musing over memories that touched on this very question. "When I was a new Christian, I wouldn't have known what a healthy dating relationship was if it hit me square in the face," my friend said with uncommon candor. Most of us can identify with her response because we've been so contaminated by the world's counterfeit that we no longer recognize God's design.

The Cornerstone

Individual dating is most beneficial between people who have the same basic outlook—not just two Christians, but two Christians who have committed their lives to God. The Bible is the source for determining truth in every area of our lives—dating, courtship, and marriage included. However, since dating is a twentieth-century phenomenon, Scripture stakes out for us only the parameters for our behavior. We know unequivocally, for instance, that God designed sex for marriage (Hebrews 13:4), and that our relationships should be others-centered (Philippians 2:3).

But inside those boundaries, there's much room for discussion. There are almost as many opinions of what dating should be like among Christians as there are speakers to address the topic. The opinions range from being a "neverdater" to actively shopping for a mate.

The neverdater harbors the misconception that one day he'll open his Bible, a verse will capture his attention, and he'll feel led to propose marriage by letter to a girl he had coffee with at a conference three years earlier! God can work in your life in that way if he wants to, but it's certainly not the norm.

On the other end of the spectrum, there is the guy who takes Sally bowling on Friday, Brenda to a picnic on Saturday, and Kathy to church on Sunday. He's probably dating solely for the purpose of marrying, and the sooner the better.

May we present some principles for a healthy, balanced view of dating and relating to the opposite sex that fall somewhere between these two extremes?

Important Reasons to Date

What's right for you socially at one point in your life may not be right at another time. However, healthy relationships with the opposite sex can serve some very productive purposes in your life.

To Develop Socially

How well do you remember your first date? For most of us that event was marked by sweaty palms, a nervous stomach, and awkward silences.

Thankfully, those distressing symptoms lessen in time, though few of us become anxiety-free overnight. James Curran, an associate professor of psychiatry at Brown University, reported that dating anxiety was the leading reason why the students he studied sought counseling. Characteristically, they had an "unrealistic perception of what occurs on dates so they can never live up to their expectations."[1] It seems that knowing how to plan for a date, what to say and do, and how to initiate and maintain conversation can sometimes present themselves as overwhelming obstacles.

Not long ago we had an intriguing evening studying the dynamics of a socially awkward situation. Some graduates of a military institution took us and some of the girls in our college ministry out to dinner. These guys were so ill at ease that most of the evening's conversation consisted of a steady stream of old military jokes. The girls listened politely, but you could tell this was hardly the most stimulating conversation they'd participated in all week. As we discussed it later, we marked that experience down as a graphic illustration of social immaturity.

A person can have a consistent walk with God, be well read, play a mean racquetball game, and yet be socially crippled. Social awkwardness is usually rooted in the soil of insecure self-confidence and lack of understanding of the differences between guys and girls. This awkwardness can be overcome with time and experience.

Christ developed socially over a period of time. He "grew in wisdom and stature, and in favor with God and men" (Luke 2:52). Learning to relate socially to the opposite sex is basically just developing people skills. It means being comfortable enough yourself to make others feel at ease, and learning to draw out another person.

Healthy dating relationships allow you to appreciate the differences between you and someone of the opposite sex in a pure sense. When asked what she appreciated most about a healthy dating relationship, one girl replied, "I value a guy's objectivity. It lifts me out of the muddle of my own emotional thinking." Likewise guys often report that a woman's perspective sensitizes them to emotions and feelings. One said, "When Cheryl shared with me her frustrations with the way I analytically disected everything, her feelings provided the needed motivation to rechannel that tendency."

God can greatly broaden your social horizons as you view life through the eyes of the opposite gender. In the long run, you'll be better equipped with more of the sensitivity and communication skills vitally necessary for a healthy social life as an adult, whether married or single.

To Have a Good Time

Debbie had really been looking forward to this evening. Since she'd trusted Christ, her dating life had been in transition, and Phil was one of the first Christian guys to ask her out. The actual event was not, however, what she had anticipated.

During the course of one short evening, Phil asked her how many children she wanted, what verses she was memorizing, who she had witnessed to recently, and whether or not she was interested in the mission field. He took her to tour the building that housed the offices for his graduate work, and then announced that he really couldn't afford to buy her a coke and sit and talk. When she returned home that evening, Debbie's comment was, "You know, an evening like that is enough to drive me back to dating non-Christians."

It wasn't that Debbie didn't want to share her memory verses or visit the graduate school building. Not at all! What she missed during the evening was spontaneity and fun. She didn't want to be approached as a project, but rather as a person whose affinity for canoeing was as important as her ability to do Bible study.

To say that dating among Christians should be different from dating among non-Christians is not to say it should be boring and intensely serious. In fact, quite the opposite is true. God has richly given us all things for our enjoyment (1 Timothy 6:17), not the least of which are our relationships with other Christians. If anybody is able to have genuine fun, it's the Christian, for several reasons.

Greater commonality. When Adam and Eve sinned, their fallen state affected not only their relationship with God but also their relationship with each other. They used fig leaves to symbolically hide from each other. Conversely, when we're restored to God through Jesus Christ, we can experience an openness, honesty, and intellectual intimacy not possible before.

When we approach God, we're not merely concerned with what he can do for us or give to us. He is a *personality* who can be known, not just an ethereal Santa Claus who satisfies our desires. We fall in love with his character, his personality. Similarly, when you're freed from seeking sensual pleasure in a relationship with another person, his or her total personality is opened to you in a new way. It's that very potential for deeper communication that provides the basis for enjoying another person.

Many people say that the biggest factor in their desire to date only Christians is that relationships with non-Christians seem shallow by comparison. Christians can relate on the plane of the permanent and lasting as opposed to the surface and transitory. Conversation becomes more than just idle chitchat.

Two Christians have infinitely more in common than two unbelievers. We are citizens of two distinct worlds that interrelate: we can talk of life as it is now with our hobbies, opinions, and routines; and life as it is yet to be in the dimension of eternity. This presents endless possibilities for conversation. There are really not many excuses for two Christians to have a boring evening.

Potential for genuine acceptance. When she was in college, a friend of mine had to pass a fraternity house every day. The guys living there sat on the porch and called out a number from one to ten, depending on their evaluation of the girls walking by. Occasionally my friend was disgusted enough to retaliate with her own number system!

Conversely, it's the absence of judgmental evaluation and the presence of unconditional acceptance that marks relationships among Christians as fundamentally different. The climate of mutual acceptance is absolutely essential to enable someone to really relax around another person and feel as comfortable as he does with his own family. As Christians we can take off our masks, acknowledging our weaknesses and failures without the fear of rejection.

(It's true that even as Christians many people do not experience the acceptance and deeper communication that is possible in relationships. The temptation exists for one Christian to rate another from one to ten, or to defraud a person sexually or emotionally by implying commitment that's not there. Nevertheless, the potential remains for experiencing more from our relationships than if we lacked a spiritual dimension to life.)

Freedom from expectations. Much non-Christian dating behavior is motivated by the question, How can I impress you? Often this paves the way for relationships based on deceit, because a false image is projected to attract the other person. In a healthy dating relationship, each person can project his individuality unguarded, without stifling camouflage caused by undue concern over what the other person will think. What freedom to be let out of that cage!

Christians should be specialists in having a good time because they aren't suffering from the disease of undefined expectations. Or at least they shouldn't be! Being freed from the expectation of physical involvement allows you to appreciate far more than his or her big blue eyes! As one girl said, "My biggest incentive to date committed Christians is that I don't have to fight them off." The chemistry of attraction is still there (as God intended it should be), but it doesn't determine the focus of the date.

As a Christian you should also be free from laboring under the weighty expectation of "what this might lead to." Going out for an evening is not the prelude to a proposal but purely a time to relax and enjoy getting to know someone. When dating becomes more than this, it can consume your emotional energy: "What am I going to wear?" "Maybe we're meant for each other." "Did I say the wrong thing when I told her I couldn't pick her up until 8:15?" It's possible to lie awake at night stewing over such matters!

Kept in its proper perspective, healthy dating leaves you rejuvenated, able to get on with the business of living. So relax and have a good time. Learn to enjoy another person's total personality in the Lord.

To Grow in Christ

A healthy date can have the same basic effect on you as any other kind of stimulating Christian fellowship, motivating you toward love and good works (Hebrews 10:24-25). Christians are the salt of the earth. When our relationships with other Christians are what they ought to be, we should leave one another thirsting to know God better. The spiritual dynamic in a healthy dating relationship makes you more sensitive to each other and more alive to God.

Dating relationships that cause mutual spiritual growth invariably spring from radically different motivations than those of the world. As Christians, we ask, "What can I do to help you become all that God intended you to be?" Both parties are concerned with drawing the other person closer to the Lord, and that motivation determines how they dress, where they go, and what they say and do.

In a worldly perspective on dating, each person seeks to get something personally from the relationship; the guy usually seeks physical intimacy and the girl wants emotional commitment. Consciously or unconsciously, they're trying to tilt the scale in their direction to meet their own immediate desires.

The Christian and worldly perspectives on dating could be pictured like this:

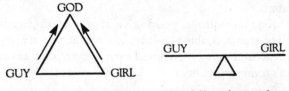

Christian relationship   **Worldly relationship**

Indeed, your motivations will have a direct effect on whether dating is a help or hindrance to your spiritual growth. No healthy dating relationship springs from the motivations of "What can I get?" and "How can I impress you?"

Much of the temptation for a Christian guy to defraud his date physically is overcome by a deepening concern for the welfare of the other person. His motivation is others-oriented rather than "What's satisfying to me." One Christian said, "When I committed my dating life to God, my eyes were opened to the value of the other person." For him, it was a fresh discovery of the unique worth of the girls he dated. If God considered them valuable enough to redeem them with the blood of Christ, then this guy could no longer exploit them for his own pleasure.

But our motivations are often difficult to identify, aren't they? One of the clearest clues for discerning your motivations is the effect the date or dating relationship is having on you. Ask yourself what it's producing in your life.

Does the relationship give you new insight into yourself and your relationship to Christ? One girl explained her growing awareness that she was expecting far too much from relationships with guys. Consequently she found more and more of her security in the Lord as she realized that no guy could meet the deeper needs of her heart. Her dating life gave her new understanding of herself and brought dramatic changes in her walk with God.

Does a dating relationship leave you with a greater motivation to obey God, to respond to his leading? Toward the end of my college days, I spent many hours over cups of coffee discussing everything from cross-cultural missions to the current world situation with a Lebanese Christian. His grasp of the Bible and culture and his contagious heart for the world ignited in me a new openness to God's leading and a desire to reach the unreached.

A date that aids your spiritual growth is much like God's word—"helpful for building others up according to their needs, that it may benefit those who listen" (Ephesians 4:29). A healthy dating relationship should give you added grace to obey God.

Pressure from Without and Within

Our culture is couple-oriented, and any single person—divorced, widowed, or never married—feels the pull to be paired up with someone. Francis Schaeffer asserts that "the man-woman relationship as God made it is the second strongest drive man had" (the first being the need to be rightly related to God.)[2]

What are the pressures that fuel the fire of this drive? Some are brought on externally by well-meaning parents and friends asking innocent questions such as "Aren't you going out this weekend?" Enough of these queries can cause you to doubt your manners, your mouthwash, and your aptitude for fun.

There's nothing quite like the solitude of an apartment or dorm room when everyone else but you has gone for a night on the town. I can also remember well the feeling of being left out as I listened to others excitedly discuss the events of the previous weekend. At times that feeling led me to a quiet desperation to be dating someone, *anyone* who cared to call.

However, as I began to focus my attention on God himself and his ability to meet my every need, he released me from that strangling pressure to be dating. When I realized the pressure I'd been feeling was cultural, I felt increasingly free to date or not to.

Other pressures originate from within the privacy of your own heart, like the longing for the security of someone committed to you. A relationship with a guy or a girl can be your self-esteem's security blanket and the panacea for your weak sense of worth. But only God can strengthen a faltering self-image—an image that is a tarnished chip of his likeness and must derive its worth from the original jewel.

If these external and internal pressures grow unchecked, finding a life partner can become a *reason* to date when instead it should be merely a *by-product* of the process. Dating can easily become a series of short shopping trips to find the right life partner. Your camera is out of focus and marriage is all you can see through its lens. Ugly emotions begin to form—lack of contentment, coveting, striving to be in a state other than the present one—and block your vision entirely.

Does this mean you can't have a healthy dating relationship and still be looking for a mate? No, not at all. But until those emotions are purified and redirected toward the Lord, your vision is clouded and you lack the discernment to choose the right life partner.

When your dependence is on the Lord and your expectation is from him, then he'll remove the frenzied quality that characterizes a fleshly search. If your foremost motivations in dating are to have a good time, to develop socially, and to grow spiritually, God will build into your life the discernment for choosing the right mate, or remove the desire.

A Glimpse at the Total Picture

As motivation for developing healthy dating relationships, consider three common dating-marriage patterns. Most people whom we have observed or counseled follow one of these. Which pattern concludes with a desirable Christian marriage? Notice the steps in the process.

The first pattern, followed by the vast majority of Christians, begins with a worldly orientation to guy / girl relationships. To some degree, they emphasize clothes, things, looks, money, prestige, and sensuality.

A few people move from this mindset and lifestyle to a period of no relationships at all with the opposite sex. During this time they may devote their energies to getting to know the Lord better and developing their ministry skills. (This is especially prevalent in a seminary situation or fast-paced ministry.)

Then at some point a relationship emerges that the person believes may involve the right one to marry. He does establish a Christian home, having married someone with the same life goals. But there are many marital adjustments, because they must learn many of the skills in relating that they could have learned before marriage through many healthy relationships.

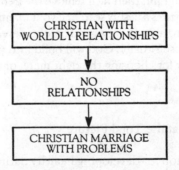

In the second pattern, which is all too common, the person proceeds from worldly, sensual relationships as a non-Christian to the same types of relationships even as a believer. Only the labels are changed! The usual result, then, is a marriage of two Christians who need their mindset and relationship revolutionized in order to have a marriage that's distinctively Christian and honoring to the Lord.

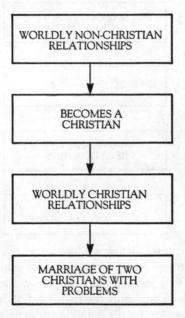

The third pattern involves a broad exposure to many healthy relationships usually produces the most satisfying marriage. In this pattern, basic relational skills are learned prior to marriage. This process provides time to mature and establish criteria for choosing a life partner. It also provides the opportunity to establish good communication skills prior to marriage. Finally, from a wealth of many relationships, one person with like mind and heart is chosen.

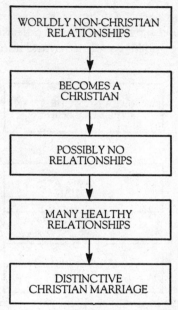

In our culture, dating is a forerunner of and preparation for marriage. Many patterns learned as an apprentice follow you, for good or for ill, into your own marital shop. Thus it follows that only the right kind of dating is adequate preparation for the right kind of marriage. Healthy dating relationships breed healthy marriages.

Notes 1. As reported by Marilyn Machlowitz in "Anxiety Still Surrounds U.S. Dating Practices," *Stillwater News Press*, 19 May 1981, page 8.

2. Francis Schaeffer, in the foreword to *Your Half of the Apple*, by Gini Andrews (Zondervan, 1972), page 1.

Questions for Personal Study and Application

1. How do you think the world defines a date?

2. From your own experience, what typifies the normal dating relationships of the world?

3. According to the following passages, how are two Christians to relate to each other?
   a. Our *attitudes*: Romans 12:10; Romans 14:13; Ephesians 4:2
   b. Our *actions*: Romans 14:19; Galatians 5:13; Galatians 6:2
   c. Our *speech*: Colossians 3:9; Colossians 3:16; 1 Thessalonians 5:11

4. The authors suggest that there are some general differences between men and women.
   a. What are the authors' ideas?
   b. What are some of your own observations?
   c. How should your awareness that there are differences affect your actions and conversation?

5. According to the authors, and from your own personal experience, what are some ways guys and girls try to impress each other on a date? How can a Christian avoid this temptation?

6. What are some of the external and internal pressures to date that you experience? How do you cope with them?

7. Which of the three dating-marriage patterns is closest to your experiences so far? If there is a need to change your pattern, what steps should you take?

8. What is one area of your dating life that you feel God wants you to change? How will you go about it?

Scripture memory assignment: Memorize one verse listed in question three.

Special project: Ask several Christians how they would describe a healthy date.

Questions for Discussion

Question 1: How do the authors define a date? How would you change that definition, if at all? What do you think are the advantages and disadvantages of one-to-one dating and group dating?

Question 2: Why should the dating relationship between two Christians be different? What are the reasons suggested for why Christians can have an especially good time on a date?

Question 3: Additional verses to read are Romans 12:16 and 15:7, Ephesians 4:31, and Hebrews 3:13. What are practical examples of ways to apply these verses in dating situations?

Question 4: How might these specific differences affect a date, and how should you respond to them?

Question 5: Do you think these efforts to impress are deceitful? Why? How should you respond if you think your date is trying to impress you in an unnatural way?

Question 8: Summarize what you feel are the marks of a healthy date.

4
Responsibilities

> There are three things that are too amazing for me,
> four that I do not understand:
> the way of an eagle in the sky,
> the way of a snake on a rock,
> the way of a ship on the high seas,
> and the way of a man with a maiden. (Proverbs 30:18)

LIKE AN EAGLE or a snake or a ship, a relationship between a man and woman is at once a mysterious and a beautiful thing. It's much like watching the characters in a drama—except that it's real life! Each person has unique lines to say and a complementary part to play in the life of the other. The unfolding of each character determines whether you view a masterpiece production or a failure.

And yet we live in a world that seems hellbent to erase the distinctions between male and female. The uniqueness of being a man or a woman is somehow being lost in the shuffle to find equality between the sexes. But those identities are not interchangeable. To blur and nullify their distinctiveness is, as Elisabeth Elliot points out in her book *The Mark of a Man*, to deprive the sexes of their glory.[1] In a similar vein, Walter Trobisch says, "The woman can only be a woman as long as a man is a man. And the man can only be a man as long as a woman is a woman. When you even out the differences, you deprive them both."[2]

The question posed for us today is, Does sexuality mean anything more than biology? It means, for one thing, that there is something about being male or female, created in us by God, that influences the way we think and act. Granted, the differences between the sexes may be elusive; they are not easily expressed with words. But that does not make them any less real.

These differences in men and women are true in *general*; they are not rigid stereotypes. They can add spice, intrigue, and sometimes frustration to a dating situation. They also explain why a man and woman can form an unbeatable combination when they each capitalize on the other's unique orientation to life. For this reason we will examine the unique contributions made by a girl and a guy.

Especially for Women

"I think our Christian task," Walter Trobisch writes, "is to teach or to show the emancipated woman how to regain or to keep her womanliness. . . . She needs to be told that she will only be respected, not as a masculine female which is exactly what men will despise, but by being a woman, completely woman, emancipated, but a woman."[3]

Both before and during marriage, a man needs to be complemented by those unique traits that are usually a woman's. As a woman, you should appreciate and accentuate the feminine qualities God has given you. They're yours for a purpose.

The Potential to Complement

It is a woman's distinctive orientation to life that makes her the attractive complement to a man. Generally speaking, women pay more attention to detail and are intuitive by nature, picking up the subtle nuances, gestures, and connotations often missed by the male gender. They usually have a more sensitive, emotional, subjective outlook on life.

Men tend to be specialists at analyzing the big picture, They are usually more objective and direct, heading straight for the point. They don't care about all the details—just the necessary information.

Picture George and Sarah eating dinner with another couple in a restaurant. Sarah wonders, Why aren't they getting along tonight? There's too much tension in the air. George's attention is fixed on one thought—the movie starts at 7:30. How can I get this group through here faster, so we can get to the movie on time? George could profit by Sarah's sensitivity to the emotionally charged atmosphere; and Sarah must realize that the movie will start at 7:30, with or without them.

By your openness. If you ask a guy what it is about going

out with a girl that really stimulates his growth and challenges his walk with God, invariably he will say, "when she just shares what God's doing in *her* life." The female version of open and honest sharing seems to be one of the greatest incentives for a person's spiritual growth. God has given you a tremendous opportunity to be the spiritual spark plug.

By your responsiveness. "The purposes of a man's heart are deep waters, but a man of understanding draws them out" (Proverbs 20:5). Likewise, a woman can be of tremendous help and encouragement to a man by drawing out his thoughts and ideas (and vice versa I might add). Your honest feedback, expressed with the kindness spoken of in Proverbs 31:26 (NASB) can help him refine and crystallize his ideas.

Men differ one from another in their tolerance of challenge from a woman, and it is well to remember that a man's ego can be fragile. A guy needs your suggestions and ideas, not a grilling cross-examination or a barrage of personal opinions. He needs someone to stimulate his thinking, to be incentive for his right responses—not someone who whittles away at all his ideas.

A woman functions best in her relationship with a man by complementing, not competing with, his ego.

The Potential to Captivate

More than 2500 years ago a wise man wrote, "I find more bitter than death the woman who is a snare, whose heart is a trap, and whose hands are chains" (Ecclesiastes 7:26). The author who penned that was Solomon, a veritable authority on women with 700 wives and 300 concubines (1 Kings 11:3). Of course, he might not have found the nature of women to be snares and traps had he stuck to pleasing only one of them.

As we grow in spiritual maturity, most of us become only too aware of our tendency to manipulate a man; in effect, to lay a snare for him. One girl said to me, "You know, periodically it devastates me to see the extent of my power to bewitch and ensnare guys I go out with. God has opened my eyes to a huge flaw in my character."

What motivates us in this peculiar ability to ensnare a guy, and how do we exercise this deadly art? I think that the root cause is our desire to have someone particularly interested in *us*. We enjoy being pursued. It does something for us to think that we can totally capture a guy's attention and maneuver him to do things he might not do in a more rational state.

This overwhelming urge to have someone particularly interested in her often leads a girl to exchange physical intimacy with a guy for even fleeting feelings of closeness and love. As the saying goes, "Guys give love to get sex. Girls give sex to get love."

Illustrations of this are all too common, but one is particularly vivid in my memory. I had worked with Kelly for two years in basic follow-up and Bible study after she became a Christian, and the time came to encourage her to commit herself to a church singles group. The one that Kelly picked was not the group I might have chosen for her, but she got involved and I didn't see much of her for a year or so.

One day she appeared at my door with a face so drawn I wondered what the teaching profession was doing to her. I invited her in and expected her to tell me what a difficult group of children she had in her class, but her actual story left me in shock for days. Kelly had been living with a guy she met in the singles fellowship. He promised to marry her that summer, and then walked off with another unsuspecting girl a month before the promised wedding.

Kelly was an attractive, down-to-earth, wholesome girl and not a likely candidate for moving in with a guy. But the stark reality of pushing thirty caused her to panic, and she exchanged sex in a desperate attempt to gain love, marriage, and commitment. Sad to say, she not only didn't find love and commitment, but she was devastated from the attempt. This is often the case when a woman seeks to bind a man's affection to her; in attempting to captivate him, she herself is capsized.

There are other ways that women use to get commitment from a guy, short of actually going to bed with him. Three that the Scriptures mention or imply are our words, our eyes, and our dress. These devices are so common in our twentieth century culture that you may not have really considered them before.

Our words. Proverbs speaks clearly of "the strange woman . . . the adulteress who flatters with her words" (Proverbs 2:16, NASB). She has a "smooth tongue" (6:24) and flattering lips with which she seduces her prey (7:21). Now we don't like to think of ourselves as adulterous women just because we use flattery, but God says it's a practice that deceives men and leads them astray. Webster defines the word *flatter* as, "to praise excessively especially from motives of self-interest; to raise the hope of or gratify especially by false . . . representations."[4] That's almost as convicting as Scripture!

Sometimes there is also a subtle temptation in communication for a woman to build "emotional bridges."

Discussing future plans, sounding out his ideas about marriage and children, and attempting to counsel his problems can be used to turn a man's eyes toward marriage prematurely. "His mouth speaks from that which fills his heart" (Luke 6:45, NASB); thus if a woman allows God to free her heart from an obsession with marriage, her speech is usually free of implications of a permanent relationship.

Our eyes. Our little girl, Allison, is a miniature case study in a woman's innate ability to use her eyes to her advantage. As soon as Allison could smile at three months, she could simultaneously bat those eyelashes, especially at her daddy! There have been times when I thought he might jump down the chimney like Santa Claus if that were her plea.

What I observed in Allison is common to her mother and, for that matter, to most women. The Bible doesn't advocate that we retreat behind dark sunglasses, but it does reveal that we can use our eyes destructively as a tool to ensnare. Solomon warns his son not to let the immoral woman captivate him with her eyes (Proverbs 6:25). We'd call such a woman a flirt because she subtly uses her eyes to entice men. It's a pitfall we should avoid.

Our dress. When I was a new Christian, I eagerly signed up for a five-week Bible study course to be held at the headquarters of a Christian organization. In my excitement I neglected to read the instructions of what to bring for the five weeks, missing altogether the fine print that said, "Only one-piece bathing suits allowed at the pool." I was rather shocked when the lifeguard (who was a girl) kindly informed me that my two-piece bathing suit wasn't allowed, and asked me to leave. I count it as one of the more embarrassing moments of my life.

At that point in my Christian life I didn't understand the reasoning behind their instructions, and I considered their rule on dress a bit Victorian. I simply didn't know what problems most guys have with their thought life and how easily stimulated they are by what they *see*. Job was obviously aware of this when he said, "I made a covenant with my eyes not to look lustfully at a girl" (Job 31:1). Jesus added the severe thought that "anyone who looks at a woman lustfully has already committed adultery with her in his heart" (Matthew 5:28).

As defined by Wayne Wright, lust is succumbing to the temptation to fulfill a valid desire in an evil way. Consider this example from Jesus' life. The first temptation that he faced in the wilderness was to command stones to become bread. There's nothing wrong with eating; it's a natural and healthy desire common to all of us. Had Jesus transformed the stones into bread at that time, though, he would have fulfilled a valid desire at the wrong time, and thus in a sinful way. Similarly, our sexual appetite, though God-given, must be satisfied within the prescribed parameter of life-long commitment to one person.

Noticing that a woman looks lovely is not lust. As Billy Graham says, "Lust is the *second* look," going beyond that innocent glance to raw desire and allowing it to occupy your mind.

For a guy, what he sees can be the springboard to lust in his mind which can give birth to sin in an overt act. A survey taken among 5,000 guys who had participated in premarital sex showed that the number one stimulus for them was a girl in a tight sweater or a revealing blouse. Obviously, what they saw didn't just go "in one eye and out the other."

Motivation to dress discreetly is rooted not only in a girl's desire for modesty but also in an understanding of a guy's perspective and limitations. My consideration for how I dress is like many other areas of Christian liberty. I am free to dress as I like, but I choose to limit my freedom in deference to my brother. Romans 14:13 admonishes, "Make up your mind not to put any stumbling block or obstacle in your brother's way." I *am* my brother's keeper in that I should dress in a way that will not hinder his spiritual growth. Beyond that, he is responsible for his thought life.

Ask God to give you an overriding concern for the spiritual welfare of the guys you're around, and to free you from those subtle ulterior motives to capture their attention for yourself.

Elisabeth Elliot says that she is often asked the question, What can I do to get him to notice me? Note carefully the advice she gives.

> My answer is "nothing." That is, nothing toward the man.
>
> Don't call him. Don't write a little note with a smiley face or a flower or a fish under the signature and put it in his campus mailbox. Don't sidle up to him in the hall and gasp, "I've just got to talk to you!" Don't look woebegone, don't ignore him, don't pursue him, don't do him favors, don't talk about him to nine carefully selected listeners.
>
> There is one thing you can do: turn the whole business over to God. If he's the man God has for you, "no good thing will he withhold from those who walk uprightly" (Psalm 84:11).
>
> Direct your energies to obedience, not to nailing the man. God has his own methods of getting the two of you together. He doesn't need any help or advice from you.[5]

"Charm is deceptive, and beauty is fleeting; but a woman who fears the Lord is to be praised" (Proverbs 31:30). As we truly reverence God, he will give us the ability to complement rather than captivate a man. Only God can make each of us the glory of some man—if that is his plan—who will in turn bring glory to the Master Designer (1 Corinthians 11:7).

Especially for Men

Many women feel that men have it made. As men, we can choose whom we take out, where we take them, how much we'll spend, and whether or not we'll call again. There are many variables over which we have much of the control, and with that control comes responsibility. The choices that we make reveal our motivation and mindset toward women—either a desire to contribute to their growth or a desire to conquer and control them.

The Desire to Contribute

A guy in a dating situation is somewhat analogous to ice cream that is yet to be frozen. In the context of marriage, he will function as the loving leader of his home. In a dating situation, he is not the spiritual leader in the same sense; he has all the ingredients but he isn't the finished product yet!

The concept of a guy as the spiritual leader gives birth to many misconceptions about his role in a dating relationship. It can cause him to view a girl as a project to be discipled. One girl expressed it this way: "I still feel like an object around some Christian guys. Before I was a Christian, guys treated me as an object in a sensual sense. Now, some of them approach me as a spiritual object—a project to be developed, not a person to be enjoyed."

To discern whether or not you have any misconceptions about your role in a dating relationship, ask yourself some questions. Do you really feel you can learn from a girl—be challenged and changed by her thinking and insight? Do you find yourself trying to put in the last word in the conversation, as though somehow you must always have the greater flash of insight?

The New Testament tells us that we are all members of one another irrespective of our sex (Romans 12:5). As such, "the eye cannot say to the hand, 'I don't need you!'" (1 Corinthians 12:21). In other words, you need a girl's opinions and views. You have an incomplete picture without them.

By assuming responsibility. You must decide whom you'd like to take out. When you're contemplating the possibilities, consider more than physical features—there's much more to girls than what you see. It's all too easy to want to date a girl who will make you look good. (Women aren't immune to that temptation either.)

Even though as men we tend to look at the outward appearance, we should look at the heart, as God does (1 Samuel 16:7). Consider this question: If you were blind, whom would you be attracted to; whom would you want to take out? The answer to that question tells you which girls you're attracted to on the basis of their inner character qualities.

In a dating situation, you voluntarily take on the responsibility for the welfare of the girl. The first summer that I knew Paula, I was working on a construction site as a carpenter. After being there a few weeks, I began to take great pains to prevent Paula from exposure to the atmosphere, conversation, and bulging eyeballs. On an actual date, you should treat that girl the way you'd treat the girl you eventually marry.

When you're designing a date, keep in mind what effect you want to leave on the person you take out. If you want to sit back and be wholesomely entertained, then choose a movie or play or ballgame or whatever will accomplish just that. If you want to discuss an idea, exchange stories from the past, or find out about her particular interests, then plan a time and place for that purpose. Paula and I usually keep a running list of every place in town that serves an endless pot of coffee. Whatever you do, remember the goal is to have a good time and to encourage each other in the Lord.

Perhaps a word of caution from Proverbs is appropriate: "A prudent man sees danger and takes refuge, but the simple keep going and suffer for it" (Proverbs 22:3). One friend of ours was very embarrassed when he had to get up with his date and leave a movie whose rating he'd forgotten to check. Like Daniel who "resolved not to defile himself" (Daniel 1:8), think ahead to situations that could be potentially compromising or sensually stimulating and avoid them.

By communicating. Have you ever sat in a restaurant and observed married couples? It's usually a study in eyes that don't meet and conversation that doesn't take place. In fact, Paula and I often feel conspicuous as we drape over cups of coffee intensely batting around some idea. But communication skills don't come naturally for many men. They must be developed, and a dating situation is an ideal place to begin.

Communication specialists tell us that there are five levels in communication. John Powell, well-known writer on interpersonal relationships, explains them as follows:

Level 5—cliché conversation
Level 4—reporting the facts about others
Level 3—my ideas and judgments
Level 2—my feelings (emotions)
Level 1—peak communication (real understanding and identification)[6]

Until you've progressed to level three, you really haven't had a much more significant conversation than speaking to a stranger on the street.

In an effort to reach a deeper level of communication, guys will commonly proceed too rapidly. The result is inappropriate questions and awkward conversation. One example of this in chapter three was the illustration in which Phil asked Debbie how many children she wanted before he knew how her day was!

In a typical dating situation, the levels of communication may work something like this.

George: Tell me what a typical day is like in your classroom. (Level 5—cliché conversation)

Eleanor: Well, on a good day you could walk into my classroom and find most of the kids working quietly at their desks, and me helping one or two on the side. On a bad day, like a rainy Friday or the week before Christmas, they might be swinging from the ceiling. (Level 4—reporting the facts)

George: What do you think is going to happen in the teaching field? Do you see yourself staying in that profession? (Level 3—ideas and judgments)

> Eleanor: You asked me a sensitive question. I've
> been feeling that maybe the Lord is directing
> me into school counseling where I could work
> with one student at a time. Trying to control a
> room-full of students is becoming a real emo-
> tional drain. I just don't feel adequate for it
> anymore. (Level 2—feelings and emotions,
> which broke through to level 1—open, total
> sharing with all defenses down)

This example is not to imply that you can progress through all five levels by asking two questions! But notice that the questions George asked did not have one-word answers.

Sometimes we mistakenly think of communication in a social situation like dating as no more than "just making conversation." To be sure, surface conversation about im-mediate events ("Who won the game?") and common friends ("Did Bill tell you what happened at his office?") has its place. But don't stop there.

It's also important as a guy that you make a real effort to relate on an emotional level to the girls around you—not just discuss the hard, cold, objective facts. Communicating on the deeper levels of attitudes, values, habits, and outlook is the most crucial skill to develop.

An older man once said to me that he'd come to a startling realization. "Fifty percent of the world (and not just women) has an emotional orientation to life. So if I want to learn to communicate effectively, I must be able to relate on an emotional plane." When you ask someone how she feels about something, as opposed to just what happened or her opinion of the situation, you com-municate real concern for her as a person.

In order to really understand someone, you must become a student of his or her non-verbal cues as well. What message is he or she giving you through gestures, expressions, and body language? Studies show that women are much better decoders of non-verbal communication than men. We have a lot to learn!

The tendency for most guys is to communicate with touch rather than words. In fact, those whose dating backgrounds are steeped in sensuality find themselves retarded in their ability to communicate with words alone. Generally speaking, the more a couple delves into the sensual before marriage, the less able they become to communicate verbally. But getting to know a body has nothing to do with getting to know the person inside that body. Inability to communicate with a woman as a total person can spell disaster in a marriage. For this reason, talking should replace physical interaction in a healthy dating situation.

By developing sensitivity. When is the last time you asked, "Are you angry with me?" or said, "I just learned something new about myself," or admitted, "I feel nervous about interviewing for this new job"? It's acceptable to discuss someone's emotions or admit your own only if you're a woman. For a man, feelings are sometimes similar to roaches—disgusting and something to get rid of. A man who is insensitive and unaware of his emotional needs will often be quite callous to the feelings of those around him, especially women. What heartache this can breed.

Not long ago I asked Eleanor if she was still going out with a guy she'd dated frequently. "Well, I guess you could say that relationship is at a standstill," she replied. "Dick announced last week that he didn't think our relationship was clicking and we shouldn't go out anymore."

"Did you talk through the whys and wherefores and come to some mutual understanding?" I asked.

"No, we didn't," she replied with a note of bitterness in her voice. "He didn't ask what I thought or felt, and I didn't say. He's the leader in this situation, you know."

Here the macho image was insensitively imposed upon the concept of leadership, with a resulting case of misunderstanding. No doubt this was an unpleasant topic for Dick to approach, but Eleanor might have been more understanding and less angry had he just talked the matter through and asked, "How do *you* feel about this, Eleanor? I value your opinion."

We're suffering from an overdose of the macho man—competitive, aggressive, and assertive. He really needs no one. He says what he thinks—bluntly and sharply—or says nothing at all.

Contrast this image with Jesus Christ, the most sensitive, caring man who ever lived, yet a truly masculine man. It wasn't incompatible for him to angrily turn over money tables in the temple, address the Pharisees as a brood of vipers and hyprocrites, and yet be found weeping at Lazarus's tomb. On the night of his suffering in Gethsemane, he unabashedly requested the support of his disciples: "Stay here and keep watch with me" (Matthew 26:38). Even more amazing, we're told that Christ, who made the universe, was "touched with the feeling of our infirmities" (Hebrews 4:15, KJV). He felt for us and with us.

Biblical sensitivity is others-centered. In a dating situation that means you should be sensitive to a girl's needs, feelings, preferences, and opinions. Neither Marvin Milquetoast or Richard Roughshod, you are moved by your own feelings and someone else's too.

The Desire to Conquer

In our culture, we grow up with a perverted view of manliness that equates maturity with sexual appeal and conquest. Few of us are immune to this pressure. As one guy said to me, "By the time I was a freshman in college, I could always expect the guys to ask me if I was sleeping with the girl I was currently dating. Any kind of purity was puritanical and weak."

Moving to a biblical perspective on guy/girl relationships requires a radical shift of mindset. Any guy (or girl for that matter) previously involved in a sensual relationship must make a clean break with the past. There are wounds to be healed, a conscience to be reshaped, a mind to be overhauled. Even though sin is forgiven, its consequences are real. As Proverbs 6:28 reminds us, "Can a man walk on hot coals without his feet being scorched?"

Chapter seven, "Celibacy in a Sexy World," explains how to experience God's total forgiveness and achieve victory in this area of sensuality. God's plan is that "each of you should learn to control his own body in a way that is holy and honorable" (1 Thessalonians 4:4). We can trust the Lord to give us a lifestyle of purity and a motivation to contribute rather than sexually conquer and defraud.

Emotionally. As men we must be even more sensitive to implying commitment we really don't feel. (Again this isn't limited to guys.) The practice of "stringing her along" can result from an insecure personality trying to control the affections of another person, or it can be quite innocent. You just didn't realize that when you sent her roses, took her out six weekends in a row, and asked her home to meet your folks that she'd begin to make wedding plans!

A dating relationship should be well defined. When in

doubt, or if you think the girl is, spell it out. If you sense that a girl you're dating is hoping for more commitment in a relationship than you feel, you owe it to her to talk honestly about your feelings. It's an immature, unfair solution to simply stop dating her and "let her figure it out."

Thinking It Over

No doubt as you are reading this chapter you are thinking, "But I know women who do that too" or "That's equally true for guys." You're right. Some of the differences between men and women overlap—those differences are *real* but not *rigid*. But as one counselor said, "So much of life can be explained when you accept that men and women think and respond in different ways." Awareness of the distinctive traits of being male or female can help you modify your behavior and accept the behavior of the other person.

Notes 1. Elisabeth Elliot, *The Mark of a Man* (Fleming Revell, 1981), page 32.

2. Walter Trobisch, "Lovestyle," *His*, February 1975, page 25.

3. Trobisch.

4. *Webster's New Collegiate Dictionary* (G. & C. Merriam Company, 1974), page 437.

5. Elisabeth Elliot Gren, "Whatever happened to dating?" *Moody Monthly*, July-August 1978, page 70.

6. John Powell, *Why Am I Afraid to Tell You Who I Am?* (Argus Communications, 1969), pages 54–61.

Questions for Personal Study and Application

We encourage you to complete all the questions because of what you could learn about the opposite sex.

Especially for Women
1. Describe our culture's concept of a woman's role in dating. How does your concept differ?

2. Read 1 Peter 3:3–4. What are the aspects of appearance that women should be concerned about?

3. Look up the following verses that reveal some positive and negative character traits of women. Identify the characteristic and its effect.
   Positive: Proverbs 11:16; 19:14; 31:25
   Negative: Proverbs 2:16–19; 9:13; 27:15–16

4. What are the differences between flattery and a sincere compliment?

Especially for Men
5. Describe our culture's concept of a guy's role in dating. How does your concept differ?

6. How would you describe spiritual leadership in a dating relationship? How has the spiritual leader role been abused in dating and marriage?

7. What are some ways that guys are insensitive to their dates?

8. Write down one principle for planning from each verse: Proverbs 14:22; 16:3; 19:2; 21:5.

9. List one potential date activity for each of the following types: entertainment, sports, hobbies, education, spiritual growth. What will be the objective and the atmosphere for each one?

For Both Men and Women
10. The authors write about John Powell's five levels of communication on page 59: level 5—cliché conver-

sation; level 4—reporting the facts; level 3— my ideas and judgments; level 2—my feelings; level 1—peak communication. Indicate the levels of communication that are appropriate for the following levels of commitment: one date; casual dating; serious dating; engagement; marriage.

11. Why should you keep a dating relationship well defined?

12. What one or two applications will you make of ideas gained from this study?

Scripture memory assignment: for women; 1 Peter 3:3-4
for men; Proverbs 22:3

Special project: Share your applications from this study with one or two close friends. Ask them if they see a greater need in your dating life, and how to meet that need.

Questions for Discussion

Question 1: Do you agree with the authors that a woman's role is that of complementing a man, rather than competing with him? Why or why not?

Question 2: What attitude should women have toward the external aspects of their appearance? How would you paraphrase this passage?

Question 3: How have you seen women manipulate men?

Question 4: Describe a hypothetical conversation in which a girl uses flattery to manipulate a guy she is interested in.

Question 5: What do you think is a man's most important role or responsibility on a date?

Question 6: Is leadership something the man has, or is it something the woman gives him? Do men usually feel they can learn spiritually from women? Can you give an example of a spiritual lesson learned through a woman?

Question 7: Do you feel the guy has to make all the decisions in a dating relationship? Why or why not? What are some ways guys can be more sensitive to women?

Question 8: Why is it important to plan ahead for a date? Can you give an example of the results of thorough planning and poor planning for a date?

Question 9: What other types of dates can you think of?

Question 11: How would you go about defining a dating relationship? How do guys sometimes falsely communicate commitment to women, whether or not it is intentional?

5

Dating with Discernment

LET'S LISTEN IN on a conversation between Darius Demon and his understudy. They are discussing the fate of Joe.

> Darius: What have you been doing for the last two weeks? I've just received word that Joe has joined the ranks of the enemy—and I can't stand listening to that party those angels are throwing.

> Understudy: I did the best I could, but the enemy out-maneuvered me.

> Darius: Well, no use crying over repenting pagans! Fall back on plan number two. See if you can get

Joe interested in Michelle—that girl who works in his office. She's been firmly entrenched in our camp now for years. With a little of our help, maybe she can draw Joe's heart away from the enemy before he gets his feet too firmly planted. Now get on it!

This is a rather humorous anecdote unless you've been faced with Joe's temptation—to date an unbeliever—and perhaps have done so. At one time or another, many of us have been caught in this dilemma, and only increased doses of discretion and self-control prevented a more permanent mismatch.

Dating non-Christians is an emotion-packed subject with far-reaching implications. To those who have not considered the question before (new Christians, for example), it seems discriminatingly narrow and far too radical to limit the field from which you choose or accept dates. But we ask you to hear out the case we plead: date with discretion and assure yourself of a like-minded marriage partner if you marry.

Being Unequally Yoked with an Unbeliever

Marriage was designed for oneness—two personalities woven together by the harmony of like-mindedness. Being unequally yoked is a marital masquerade in which unity and oneness become unattainable goals. Keeping the principle of oneness in mind will help you understand why Scripture speaks so dogmatically about who you marry, and thus, who you date.

Do not be yoked together with unbelievers. For what do righteousness and wickedness have in common? Or what fellowship can light have with darkness? What harmony is there between Christ and Belial! What does a believer have in common with an unbeliever? What agreement is there between the temple of God and idols? For we are the temple of the living God. As God has said, "I will live with them and walk among them, and I will be their God, and they will be my people."

"Therefore come out from them
and be separate,

says the Lord.

Touch no unclean thing,
and I will receive you."
"I will be a Father to you,
and you will be my sons and daughters,

says the Lord Almighty."
(2 Corinthians 6:14–18)

The visual image chosen for this passage is a team of oxen that are yoked or bound together. The Corinthians understood that the Old Testament law forbid the practice of yoking together animals of different species to draw burdens (Deuteronomy 22:10). Unequally yoked animals can't plow a field efficiently because they pull in different ways and to different degrees.

At first glance this passage might appear to be without direct bearing on a dating situation. However, it addresses the question of being bound together or yoked in any kind of relationship, which would include a marriage that grows out of a dating relationship. Unequally yoked people don't make good marriage partners because they are different in important ways. Clearly, a Christian cannot marry a non-Christian and be in the will of God. There are no allowances made, no options offered, no special cases permitted. Even if the relationship never becomes a marriage, you are placing yourself under the influence of a person who, at best, will not aid your growth in the Lord.

I so appreciate God's detailed effort to explain *why* he forbids an unequal union. He refers to a Christian and a non-Christian in completely antithetical terms: light and darkness, Christ and Satan, righteousness and lawlessness, God's temple and idols. Believers and unbelievers are like oil and water—you can't successfully mix the two.

Let's look more closely at the five rhetorical questions asked in this passage to show the absurdity of a spiritually mixed marriage.

"What do righteousness and wickedness have in common?" These are fundamentally antagonistic forces that cannot be brought into a truly compatible union.

"What fellowship can light have with darkness?" None at all. The unbeliever's state now and in the future (unless he comes to Christ) is eternal darkness (Matthew 25:30). We too were once living in darkness, and now as Christians have been called out of that darkness and into God's marvelous light (Colossians 1:13, 1 Peter 2:9). There can be no real fellowship between two people living in two different spiritual conditions, destined for two different spiritual outcomes.

"What harmony is there between Christ and Belial (Satan)?" As Christians, God is our Father (Romans 8:15), and Christ is our life (Colossians 3:4). The unbeliever's father is Belial, or Satan (John 8:44). Each person, then, is controlled by a different power, and harmony is unattainable.

"What does a believer have in common with an unbeliever?" A Christian's citizenship, interest, and inheritance transcends this world. For an unbeliever, this world is the only reality he understands. Thus there's little basis for sharing the most basic issues of life.

Finally, *"what agreement is there between the temple of God and idols?"* First Corinthians 6:9-10 tells us that idolators have no part in God's kingdom. According to verse nineteen, as a Christian "your body is a temple of the Holy Spirit . . . whom you have received from God." God's temple and idols are incompatible; there can be no common purpose.

	UNBELIEVER	BELIEVER
Destiny	Eternal judgment	Eternal life
Source of power	The flesh	The Holy Spirit
Source of control	Satan	The Godhead
Status	Darkness	Light
Condition	Dead in sin	Alive in God
Allegiance	Worships false gods	Worships the true God

Use Your Imagination

The non-Christian is not in a state of neutrality. Even that moral, upstanding, nice guy is in the enemy's camp in God's sight. What are the implications of choosing a spiritually mixed marriage? For a moment imagine yourself in these hypothetical situations.

The Scripture declares that an unbeliever is spiritually *dead* (Ephesians 2:1). He has no interest and desire in spiritual things. For you as a Christian who has been given new life in Christ, further revelation of spiritual truths is life changing. To an unbelieving spouse, the same truths seem comparatively irrelevant.

Listen with me to this commonplace conversation between a believing wife and her unbelieving husband.

> Wife: Honey, did I tell you what new thought I am getting out of this women's Bible study?
>
> Husband: No, I don't think you did.
>
> Wife: Well, we've been doing this study on the Second Coming of Christ. I'd never realized that all of history will end with his return. He came the first time as a baby, and when he comes back he'll come as King. Then he'll straighten out the mess this world is in.
>
> Husband: What do you mean? Every time you read something, you learn about future solutions to our problems. New technology, advanced education, new cures for cancer—what would Christ return to save us from?

Picture this disheartened wife as she gets up to clear the breakfast table. Her honest attempt to share a new thought is thwarted; her husband just doesn't understand. As 1 Corinthians 2:14 says, "The man without the Spirit does not accept the things that come from the Spirit of God, for they are foolishness to him, and he cannot understand them, because they are spiritually discerned."

Without the presence of the Holy Spirit, a non-Christian's mind is hostile toward God and not even able to subject itself to the law of God (Romans 8:7). That manifests itself sometimes as passive indifference, but often as open opposition.

As Christians we are the fragrance of Christ "among those who are being saved and those who are perishing. To the one we are the smell of death; to the other the fragrance of life" (2 Corinthians 2:15-16). In other words, as a Christian you could actually become like a foul odor to an unbelieving mate. That's not exactly what you call a prescription for marital happiness.

How would a marriage such as this influence your relationship as husband and wife? When you became a Christian, you had the very love of God poured out into your heart (Romans 5:5). However, your mate, as an unbeliever, *cannot return it in kind*. You're thereby in a situation that forces you to give and give and give again without expecting the same affection to be returned.

The Scriptural instructions concerning marriage are the same whether you're married to a believer or an unbeliever (Ephesians 5:22-31). As a Christian husband, you must love your unbelieving wife with the same sacrificial love Christ had for the church. However, you'd be trying to maintain the spiritual leadership of your home while married to a woman who feels no obligation to respect that leadership and lend you her emotional support. And if you're a Christian wife, you'd be bound to follow the leadership of a man not tuned in to God and possibly very unresponsive to your needs.

The non-Christian's goals, prejudices, and outlook on life will be radically different from yours. You may want your husband to spend more time with the family, but he feels compelled to shoot pool three nights a week. You want to participate in a couple's Bible study, but your wife feels uncomfortable around "those people." You'd like to give sacrificially to Christian causes, but he would rather buy a deluxe swing set for the kids. There is no partnership, no harmony, no fellowship, no commonality, no agreement.

Christian author Jo Berry has likened this undesirable marriage to a father-and-son three-legged race commonly seen at picnics. Tall, bony men are tied together with short, stubby nine-year-olds, and the pairs are obviously mismatched in size, stamina, and capability. That race is always an entertaining event, but notice how quickly the pairs break apart at the end of the race. Obviously none of them would consider staying together for a lifetime, but that is the condition of a non-Christian married to a Christian. They are permanently, unequally yoked.[1]

Most pastors will agree that this problem of being unequally yoked is one of the most common that walks through their study doors. Often its roots lie buried in the dating process and indiscriminate choices made there. Two singles could not perceive the day-in and day-out reality of a half-baked marriage—one that's never quite what it was meant to be.

While a marriage of two people who know the Lord is not problem-free, there's someone you can turn to together when conflicts arise. There's an objective source of truth and guidance other than each person's own opinion and desire. What a privilege to take each disagreement, disappointment, or crisis before the Lord *together*!

The Causes of the Problem

If the consequences can be so devastating, why is the problem so common? There are at least three explanations for how this happens.

First, after two unbelievers marry, one of them

becomes a Christian. This is not really the result of indiscriminate dating, because two people with a similar spiritual condition were attracted to each other and married. Often this is an easier situation to correct because the unbelieving partner may readily see changes in the believing spouse and be motivated to consider Christ.

Sometimes a Christian marries someone he really *thought* was a Christian. Perhaps his heart was quickened before his head was enlightened and he became too emotionally involved to discern the true spiritual state of his prospective partner.

In many cases, though, a Christian begins to knowingly date an unbeliever, and when they fall in love he is unable to tear his heart away. What he thought would only be a casual date leads him to flagrantly disobey one of the most basic biblical principles of relationships. It began on a date that need never have taken place.

Did you ever consider that your choice of a date is a commentary of sorts on your spiritual state? When a Christian who is a new believer himself pursues a relationship with an unbeliever or a stagnant Christian, he is *undiscerning*. His spiritual antennae don't readily detect the differences between a Christian and a non-Christian, or even between an uncommitted Christian and a growing one.

Or possibly he is a growing Christian, but a *naive* one. The dangers and repercussions of this relationship are quickly glossed over. "A prudent man sees evil and hides himself. The naive proceed and pay the penalty" (Proverbs 27:12, NASB).

For many Christians who knowingly and willfully date unbelievers, *rebellious* more accurately describes them. They do what they want to do regardless of the consequences. Psalm 68:6 (NASB) declares, "Only the rebellious dwell in a parched land." And there's no land quite so parched as a spiritually mixed marriage of two people pulling in opposing directions.

One Case in Point

When we were newly married, Paula received a disturbing Christmas card from a girl whom she had helped grow as a Christian. Louise was the kind of girl everybody loves to lead to Christ. She studied the facts, thought it over, made a clear-cut decision for Christ, and began to grow steadily—until she met Bob. Louise assured Paula that it was a purely platonic relationship, and she had *no* intention of marrying him. All Louise knew about his spiritual condition was that he had a "church background."

But the more Louise saw of Bob, the more rapidly her spiritual interest declined until finally she was no longer interested in Bible study. Paula was not quite sure what became of Louise until she received the Christmas card three years later. Louise had married Bob and now in the more revealing light of marriage wrote, "I'm trying to teach a children's Sunday school class in a nearby church, but Bob never goes. Sometimes I think he's closer to an atheist."

If only Paula could have pointed out to Louise when she met Bob that she was entering an inevitable process leading toward her spiritual decline. The process, as outlined by Scott Kirby in his book *Dating* begins when you consider an attractive guy or girl as a potential date.[2] You may or may not know his or her spiritual condition.

You rationalize. You perform mental gymnastics to convince yourself and others that what you greatly suspect is the wrong thing to do will turn out okay. The list of rationalizations used for dating indiscriminately is endless.

"I'm just dating the guy. I have no intention of marrying him." That may be true, but plenty of people before you have contradicted those words.

"Sally says she was raised down at First Church. Someone as nice as she is would have to be a Christian." Maybe so, but there are many attractive, principled people with church backgrounds who have never personally responded to the claims of Christ.

"Well, I just don't know yet if he's a Christian or how committed he is. After all, we've only been out a few times." When I hear that comment, I have to assume that either the guy recently had his lips sewn together or she's too infatuated to listen carefully. A person's conversation is indicative of his spiritual state. If he's a Christian, how could he spend three or four hours with someone and not mention the person around whom his life revolves?

"But I just don't know many Christian guys. Who do you expect me to go out with?" Girls more often fall prey to the temptation to go out with an unbeliever or an uncommitted Christian. They have to wait to be asked out, so turning down an invitation could well mean another night without much to do. Thus Christian guys need to be sensitive to the increased temptation with which many girls wrestle. An occasional "Are you interested in taking in that basketball game Friday night" can be a big help to girls in overcoming the temptation to date just anyone.

The Christian life wasn't meant to be a solo flight; both guys and girls need stimulating fellowship with their own peer group. If your closest friends of the opposite sex are uncommitted Christians or unbelievers, then you need to break out of those circles and find some new friends. (It may not be so much a matter of dropping the old friends, as it is adding new ones.)

"Who knows—maybe I can witness to her." If you really want to share Christ with her, then introduce her to another girl who will witness to her. Most of the time when the gospel is shared cross-sexually, something is lost in the translation. The message tends to be obscured in the motives. Is she interested in coming to know Christ, or is it really you she's attracted to? If your motive really is to witness to her, you can do so without going out with her.

It certainly is not impossible to lead your date to Christ, or to influence a date strongly enough that he or she wants to become a Christian. Quite possibly you know a couple with whom that has been the case. But in most situations, it is the non-Christian who exerts the greatest influence. The danger is that you will be dragged down to his or her level, much like the process of finding the lowest common denominator.

You give in and go out. You begin to spend time with this person regularly. Possibly in the back of your mind you envision just a few casual dates, certainly not expecting something more to come of it. However, there is little hope that you can continue to go out with this person and remain unaffected by the relationship.

You fall in love. Sad, but predictable. It's the next logical step after a while. You can fall in love with any number of people. Ray Short writes that that emotion can become "a vaccine that immunizes you against seeing anything wrong with the other person."[3] You may be blinded to the spiritual state of the other person. Or you may somehow convince yourself that sooner or later he'll become a Christian and your relationship will take on that added dimension.

You must choose between that person and God. One morning a girl my wife had helped in Bible study called unexpectedly and asked if she could come over. Paula hadn't seen Carla in over a year, during which time she had apparently been riding back and forth to work with a non-Christian whom she began to date. Now she felt she was in love with him. She thought he was interested in spiritual things and that eventually he would become a Christian. He wanted to marry her in a year.

Carla was at a crossroads, faced with a very painful choice. Paula explained to her that there was no way she could continue the relationship banking on the hope that he'd become a Christian. Even if he did, he would be years behind her in spiritual understanding and maturity. Turmoil was written all over Carla's face when she left.

Essentially, if your relationship progresses to this point, you will consciously or unconsciously choose between God and that other person. Scott Kirby warns, "If you choose God, you will be hurt emotionally because you must break off the relationship. But if you choose the other person, then you will be hurt spiritually because you are putting another person before God.[4]

Rapid spiritual decline. When you willfully choose to continue an intimate relationship with a non-Christian, your heart becomes cold and indifferent to the Lord. You begin to slip back into the old grooves of your non-Christian past. And since your relationship does not have that necessary spiritual dimension, you may become physically involved. Your conscience is violated, you're burdened with guilt, and your spiritual progress comes to a screeching halt.

It is because of this inevitable spiritual decline that the Lord warns us about becoming unequally yoked. He knows that it will draw our hearts away. In Deuteronomy 7:3-4 he says, "Do not intermarry with them, Do not give your daughters to their sons or take their daughters for your sons, for they will turn your sons away from following me to serve other gods, and the Lord's anger will burn against you and will quickly destroy you." The Old Testament is filled with examples of Israel's spiritual apostasy that can be easily traced to her disobedience of this command.

Developing Discernment

The predictable process of rationalization to spiritual decline never need to take place in your life. Just don't begin to go out with someone until you know for sure that he or she is a growing Christian. Don't take his or her spiritual state for granted just because you are both members of the same youth group or singles group or college Sunday school class. Do you hear anything in your conversations that would lead you to believe he or she has a hunger to grow, a desire to know the Scriptures? Observe his or her lifestyle. Do you see evidence of availability to God, and willingness to do whatever he asks? Give the situation some time and prayer before you pick up the phone or say yes to an invitation.

What do you do if you're already in the situation of dating an unbeliever or even a Christian who's not growing? As hard as it may be, you can't be anything less than honest. The most gracious thing to do is to explain the pulled-apart tension you feel in your own heart.

In order to firmly decide that you want to date only growing Christians, you must be convinced that dating can indeed lead you to marriage, and that marriage to a non-Christian or an uncommitted Christian is not God's best for you. One African pastor warns his single people, "Go ahead and marry that unconverted person but don't come anywhere near here because I don't like to see anyone carry around a corpse."[5] Dating and marrying an unbeliever is carrying around dead weight that can prevent you from running the race that is before you, and from fixing your eyes on Jesus, the author and perfecter of that faith (Hebrews 12:1-2).

Turn back once again to 2 Corinthians 6:14-18 which forbids you to be unequally yoked. Did you notice that a wonderful promise is attached to that passage? "I will be a Father to you, and you will be my sons and daughters" (verse eighteen). In other words, he promises to fill with himself whatever void you experience. As recorded in Isaiah 30:18 (NASB), "The Lord longs to be gracious to you . . . He waits on high to have compassion on you."

Notes   1. Jo Berry, "Does Your Husband Need Jesus?" *Christianity Today*, 20 February 1981, page 28.

2. Scott Kirby, *Dating* (Baker Book House, 1979) pages 50–52.

3. Ray Short, *Sex, Love, or Infatuation* (Augsburg Publishing House, 1978), page 120.

4. Kirby, p. 52.

5. Stuart Briscoe, from the tape "A Call to Singleness."

Questions for Personal Study and Application

1. List some Christian friends and acquaintances who you think are dating non-Christians. What are the relationships like?

2. List some married friends or acquaintances who have spiritually mixed marriages; that is, a growing Christian married to a non-Christian or an uncommitted Christian. What are their relationships like?

3. Read 2 Corinthians 6:14–18.
   a. What are the differences between a Christian and a non-Christian?
   b. What are the similarities between a Christian and a non-Christian?

4. Since being a Christian is such an important fact in deciding whom to date, how do you determine who is a Christian and who is not? Be sure to include some scriptural references.

5. On pages 76–77 the authors give three explanations for why believers marry unbelievers.
   a. What are they?
   b. Think back over your dating life. If you had married a non-Christian you dated, what category would you have placed yourself in?

6. Read Deuteronomy 7:3–4. What are the implications of this passage for Christians concerning dating and marriage today?

7. On page 82 the authors list some steps for developing discernment in dating. Write down those that apply to you and list some of your own ideas as well.

8. We often fear the future. This is why we may cling to any dating relationship that comes along. Jot down some ideas from the following verses that can be applied to dating: Proverbs 3:5–6; Isaiah 26:3; Matthew 6:33.

9. Now that you have read the chapter and answered these questions, what is your present decision about dating non-Christians? Why is that your choice?

Scripture memory assignment: 2 Corinthians 6:14

Special project: Ask three or four friends what criteria they have for deciding whom to date and whom not to date. Jot down their responses and bring them to the study.

Questions for Discussion

Question 2: What differences do you see in a mixed marriage in which one partner becomes a Christian after the wedding?

Question 3: How does this passage apply to dating, and marriage that might follow?

Question 4: Do you think it is possible for a growing Christian to be fooled into thinking that a girl or guy he or she is dating is also a growing Christian? If so, how?

Question 5: What are some rationalizations that you, or those you know, have used in dating non-Christians or lukewarm Christians.

Question 6: Can you think of any Old Testament examples of a believer marrying an unbeliever?

Question 8: Who is more concerned about your future, you or God? How should that knowledge affect you?

6
Why Not?

HORNELL HART, a professor at Duke University, used to tell his classes that the survival of the human race depended on three things. "We had to (a) get our breakfast, (b) avoid being someone else's breakfast, and (c) have at least a passing interest in sex.[1]"

Most of us readily admit that our interest in sex is a trifle more than passing. Perhaps though, we've given sex an importance beyond what it deserves. According to some estimates, the average American couple spends less than one half hour per week engaged in sexual activity. While that may be quite a torrid affair, there are still 167½ hours in the week left to communicate with more than touch. Surely there must be a balance between the ascetics who view sex as degrading and the hedonists who consider pleasure to be life's summit.

Sex as It Was Meant to Be

When the *King James Version* refers to sexual intercourse, it uses the word *knew*: "Adam knew his wife Eve; and she conceived" (Genesis 4:1). Sex is a total encounter of mind, body, and spirit, far removed from the purely instinctual drive of animals. "For this cause a man shall leave his father and his mother, and shall cleave to his wife; and they shall become one flesh" (Genesis 2:24, NASB). The word *cleave* denotes the idea of "clinging to," a meshing of one's total personality with another person.

Unmistakably, sex was given for the *pleasure* of two people unreservedly committed to God and to each other. When she heard she was to have a child, Abraham's wife Sarah said, "After I am worn out and my master is old, will I now have this pleasure?" (Genesis 18:12). C.S. Lewis once pointed out that pleasure is God's invention, not the devil's.[2] He was speaking not of the Playboy pleasure that needs no justification and is only for the moment, but of a deeper version found only within the context of trust.

The Christian's view of sex also hinges on the value the Bible attaches to our physical bodies. Early Greek philosophy and even later Christian heresy (Gnosticism) held the belief that the physical world (including our bodies) was inherently evil and of little worth compared to the soul and spirit. Christianity was a radical departure from this viewpoint. The body, far from being evil, would one day be reunited with the soul and spirit, to live on in a resurrected state. As a result, while the Romans burned their dead, Christians buried theirs.

Consider the impact this teaching from 1 Corinthians 6:13, 18–20 must have had on the people of its day.

> The body is not meant for sexual immorality, but for the Lord, and the Lord for the body. . . . Flee from sexual immorality. All other sins a man commits are outside his body, but he who sins sexually sins against his own body. Do you not know that your body is a temple of the Holy Spirit, who is in you, whom you have received from God? You are not your own; you were bought at a price. Therefore honor God with your body.

Christ's atonement redeemed not only our souls but our *bodies* as well—they are not ours to do with as we please. Only Christians can appreciate their sexuality as a gift from God, to be used for his glory, while the world pays homage to the goddess of sensuality.

The Counterfeit

Sir Rabindranath Tagore once said, "I have on my table a violin string. It is free. I twist one end of it and it responds. It is free. But it is not free to do what a violin string is supposed to do—to produce music. So I take it, fix it in my violin and tighten it until it is taut. Only then is it free to be a violin string."[3] Like the violin string that performs its intended function, sexual pleasure produces its sweetest music within the limits of married love.

God always places freedom within a protective fence.

Inside those boundaries there are countless possibilities for innovation. Outside lie chaos and perversion. "It is God's will that you should be holy; that you should avoid sexual immorality" (1 Thessalonians 4:3). God's intention in placing the fence around sex is not to smother pleasure, but to *provide* and *protect* it for us.

It is common, even among Christians, to assert that premarital sex is understandable, even permissible, for a couple who plan to get married—as though once the elements of love and commitment are injected, the rules change. But there are no conditional clauses attached to the scriptural injunction to "avoid sexual immorality" or to "let the marriage bed be undefiled." The repercussions of experiencing sex before marriage are the same whether a couple plans to marry or not.

Do you remember the following lyrics? "Touch me in the morning, then just walk away. We don't have tomorrow, but we had yesterday." Those lyrics ignore the problem of illicit sex; *you can't just walk away.* You can't allow your body to experience sensual pleasure while you unplug the wires to your mind and emotions. The act of a moment has far-reaching effects on your relationship with God, your own personality, and your relationship to each other.

Your Relationship to God
"I urge you, as aliens and strangers in the world, to abstain from sinful desires, which war against your soul" (1 Peter 2:11). Sensuality is at war with the health of your soul. To give a foothold to immorality, to allow the physical drive in your life to dominate, is to place your relationship with God in neutral. Your prayers bounce off the ceiling, faith eludes you, and God seems a million miles away—until this

area is brought under the control of the Spirit.

Paul gives Timothy a concise prescription for being used of God (2 Timothy 2:14–23). He sandwiches his plea for being "an instrument for noble purposes . . . useful to the Master" between the commands "Avoid godless chatter" and "Flee the evil desires of youth." Either one can render a person spiritually sterile, useless to the Lord. A lifestyle encompassing either pitfall produces a Christian chameleon; he talks and acts so much like the natural man, you can't tell the two apart.

Your Personality

Jeff, a racquetball friend, came over for coffee recently. "How's your roommate situation?" I asked. "This guy's a Christian, isn't he?"

"He's a Christian, " Jeff said, "but he's been so depressed because his girlfriend broke up with him that his parents have been coming frequently to visit. They're afraid he's actually suicidal."

I began to probe why the loss of a girlfriend was having such a debilitating effect. Before long, the real cause surfaced. Jeff's roommate had been sleeping with his girlfriend, and when she terminated the relationship, he felt totally rejected. His mental health took a nose dive.

Dr. Mary Calderone has some views that differ from ours. However, her statement about the effect of intercourse rings true.

> There is no possibility of having sexual intercourse without meshing a part of your non-physical self. Sex is such a definite experience that a part of each of you remains forever a part of the other. How many times and how

casually are you willing to invest a portion of your total self and accept such an investment from another person, with no assurance that the investment is for keeps?[4]

"A man who commits adultery lacks judgment; whoever does so *destroys himself*" (Proverbs 6:32). In some psychological way, our body and our personal sense of worth are joined. When we share intimately with another, we give away part of our dignity (our God-given sense of nobility and honor). When we don't receive something lasting and meaningful in return, we sense that our dignity has been squandered. In a very real sense, we feel we've lost part of ourselves.

Your Relationship to Each Other
Within the bonds of marriage, sex is the most intimate seal of commitment, a tender expression of total giving that binds two people together. Outside of marriage, a focus on the physical has the opposite effect. Sex becomes a wedge, a stumbling block, a hindrance to the development of mature love. What was meant to add life and beauty to a relationship becomes, outside of marriage, the prelude to "Auld Lang Syne" for several reasons.

Sex prevents other aspects of the relationship from developing. Although the physical is the most direct route of communication and the easiest to learn, it is only the tip of the iceberg of a good relationship. Anybody can kiss, but not everyone can carry on a meaningful conversation. Often a relationship begun on a plane of physical attraction is never able to reach the deeper intimacy of the mind and the spirit.

Believe it or not, *your* skin is going to sag, and eventually you will have bulges in mysterious places—and in fewer years than you think! If someone's attraction to you is based mostly on what is sensually appealing, what kind of future does that project for your relationship? It's God's gracious intent to replace some of your physical attractiveness with a deeper inner beauty. As God develops those deeper character qualities in your life, your marriage will mature, not just endure with age. So you must think ahead to decide which aspects of your relationship will be the most important over the long haul.

Sensuality also hinders sensitivity. Often we will try to solve conflicts with a kiss or a hug, or more—rather than developing the ability to talk and pray about them. In marriage, that habit is like putting a bandage on a broken bone, leaving bitter wounds to fester, perhaps never to heal.

The qualities that hold a relationship together—trust, honesty, openness, deep friendship, spiritual intimacy—take time and effort to develop. When you focus on the physical aspect, you short-circuit that process. Physical intimacy is a mistaken attempt to quickly build emotional bridges, but relationships built on such an inadequate foundation eventually collapse. Physical attraction is simply insufficient glue with which to build or maintain a lasting relationship.

Sex injects fear and guilt into the relationship. Premarital intimacy produces guilt feelings because God has wired us together in such a way that we know we've violated his intentions. "Marriage should be honored by all, and the marriage bed be kept pure, for God will judge the adulterer and all the sexually immoral" (Hebrews 13:4). Whether an offender acknowledges God's laws or not, he feels guilty because he *is* guilty before a holy God. As Dr. Joe Aldrich says, "There is no prophylactic for the conscience."

Do you remember Pavlov's dog, which learned to associate a bell with food? Whenever he heard it ring, he began to salivate in anticipation of a meal. Premarital sex often produces an association between guilt, remorse, and fear (of pregnancy or being "found out"), and physical intimacy. This cycle of unhealthy feelings, taken into the context of marriage, is a major contributor to frigidity, impotence, and sexual maladjustment.

Sex lays a foundation of distrust and lack of respect. Mature love is built on the security of knowing that your love is exclusive. There is no one else. Premarital intimacy chips away at the cornerstone of trust as you wonder, "If he has this little control with me, maybe I won't always be the one. Maybe there were others before me." As suspicion and distrust increase, you slowly lose respect for the other person.

Sex causes you to compare one person with others. One young husband admitted that his relationship with his new wife wasn't what he had hoped it would be. "It's really my fault," he admitted. "Before we were married I had several physical relationships with girlfriends. Now whenever I kiss my wife or engage in love play, my memory reminds me that this girl could kiss better than my wife, that girl was better at something else, and so forth. I can't concentrate on loving my wife with all that I am—there have been too many women in my life to be wholly committed to one."

God can redeem this situation, but why not choose to live your life in such purity that you can wholeheartedly give yourself to one person?

Sex deceives you into thinking you're in love. Studies show that a relationship based on physical attraction may hold itself together for three to five years. During that length of time two people are fooled into thinking, "Well, we've been going together for so long, surely we can make it for a lifetime. This must be love." On the other side of marriage, they wake up to see they had little in common and no basis for a quality relationship.

If what you're feeling is merely infatuation, it will leave as quickly as it came upon you. Real love stands the test of time; it's strong enough to stand alone without the support of physical intimacy. However, if you establish a mutually satisfying sexual relationship, you lose objectivity and actually cheat on the test of time. The only way to rationally decide whether your love is for keeps is to remove any preoccupation with eros, sexual love. Otherwise you may marry a mirage, not a person you really know.

The facts are against you. In his book *Sex, Love, or Infatuation: How Can I Really Know?*, Ray Short lists some well-known, established facts about the probable effects of premarital sex on marriage.[5]

Fact 1. "Premarital sex tends to break up couples before marriage takes place."

Fact 2. "Many men do not want to marry a woman who has had intercourse with someone else." The strange logic seems to be, "It's okay for me to have sex with the girl *you* marry, but it's not okay for you to have sex with the girl *I* marry."

Fact 3. "Those who have premarital sex tend to have less happy marriages." As mentioned before, the physical relationship is an inadequate foundation upon which to build a lasting relationship.

Fact 4. "Those who have premarital sex are more likely to have their marriages end in divorce."

Fact 5. "Persons and couples who have had premarital sex are more likely to have extramarital affairs as well." This is especially true for women; those who engaged in sex before marriage are more than twice as likely to have extramarital affairs as those who did not have premarital sex.

Fact 6. "Having premarital sex may fool you into marrying a person who is not right for you. . . . Sex can blind you."

Fact 7. "Persons and couples with premarital sex experience seem to achieve sexual satisfaction sooner after they are married. However, they are likely to be less satisfied overall with their sex life during marriage." It seems that their premarital sex experiences often rise to haunt them.

There's no reasonable basis on which to defend the acceptance of premarital intimacy. God gives us his commands because he knows us all too well, and he alone knows what is best for us. John White acknowledges that "men distort Scripture because we don't like what it says—not because we've found a superior ethic."[6] As John 3:19 says, "Men loved darkness instead of light because their deeds were evil."

In the world's eyes, you may seem like a prude to choose a lifestyle of purity, but the facts supporting such a choice remain in your favor. Consider your sexuality a present from God marked "For greatest enjoyment, do not open until marriage."

Notes

1. Hornell Hart, as quoted in *Sex, Love, or Infatuation*, by Ray E. Short (Augsburg Publishing House, 1978), page 45.

2. C. S. Lewis, as quoted in *Eros, Defiled: The Christian and Sexual Sin*, by John White (InterVarsity Press, 1977), page 10.

3. Sir Rabindranath Tagore, *Leadership*, Winter 1980, Vol. 1, No. 1, page 117.

4. Mary Calderone and Eric W. Johnson, *The Family Book about Sexuality* (Harper and Row, Publishers, 1979).

5. Short, pages 83–89.

6. White, page 57.

Questions for Personal Study and Application

1. Read Genesis 2:18–24. What is God's attitude toward and purpose for sex?

2. Read 1 Corinthians 6:12–20.
   a. What is the relationship between a Christian's body and the Lord?
   b. Why is a Christian to flee from immorality?

3. According to these verses, what effect does following our lusts have on our relationship to God: Psalm 66:18; Isaish 59:2; Ephesians 5:5–6; Hebrews 13:4.

4. In what ways have you been following your lusts?

5. According to Proverbs 5:3–6 and 6:32, what are some results of premarital or extramarital sex?

6. Read Romans 13:14, Ephesians 5:3, 2 Timothy 2:22, 1 Peter 1:14, and 1 Peter 4:2–3. How should a Christian respond to lust or tempting immorality?

7. Many people have experienced premarital sex, which is sin according to the Bible. Yet God is gracious and forgiving to those who turn to him. Read Psalm 51:1–4, which reveals David's confession after his sin with Bathsheba.
   a. Whom did David really sin against?
   b. What did David ask from God?
   c. In verse fifteen, what did David resolve to do after he was forgiven?

8. What is the most important application concerning sexual purity that you can make in your life right now?

Scripture memory assignment: Ephesians 5:3

Special project: List your standards for the physical aspect of your dating relationships. Be sure to include some verse references.

Questions for Discussion

Question 1: Do Christians sometimes have attitudes toward sex that are not compatible with God's view of sex? What are some of these attitudes?

Question 2: How would you define the word *immorality* as used in this passage? What is the opposite of immorality, as stated in 1 Thessalonians 4:3-5? Read verses six through eight as well. Why has God called us? How does this passage apply to dating?

Question 3: How would you define lust? What can it be directed toward in addition to sex?

Question 4: What are some general or specific ways to overcome lust, whatever its object?

Question 5: Two more passages to read are Proverbs 2:16-19 and 9:13-18. On pages 90-96 the authors list some negative results of premarital sex. How do they compare with the passages from Proverbs? What are some traits of men and women who engage in premarital or extramarital sex?

Question 6: What does the phrase *clothe yourselves with the Lord Jesus Christ* mean (Romans 13:14)? Why should you flee youthful lusts, as commanded in 2 Timothy 2:22?

Question 7: What do you think David felt like before and after he asked God's forgiveness? How can you claim and experience forgiveness?

7

Celibacy in a Sexy World

BERT ENTERED the pastor's office as one nervous, anxious counselee and abruptly blurted out his problem. "Ginny and I have been considering and praying about marriage for some time now. Recently, though, we allowed ourselves to get in a compromising situation, and we went much further physically than either of us intended. I feel I've violated Ginny, and now I'm wondering if we should go ahead and get married."

Knowing both Ginny and Bert, the pastor asked how this could have come about. "I know you and Ginny understand why God intended sex for marriage. How, then, did your relationship progress to such a point?"

Bert shook his head and replied, "I'm really not sure, Pastor. We just never thought this would happen to us."

Most of us are well acquainted with the consequences of premarital intimacy. But knowledge itself is not sufficient motivation for sexual purity. Often our problem is a *reality gap*—a chasm between truth we know and truth we live out in our daily lives. This chapter is the bridge between principles you may already know and their application.

Harnessing Your Sexual Desires

You can't deny your sexuality or just wish it away, even if you wanted to. But you can keep it in subjection. "Each of you should learn to control his own body in a way that is holy and honorable, not in passionate lust like the heathen, who do not know God" (1 Thessalonians 4:4–5). The key word for the Christian is *control*.

For most people, mastery of their physical desires is a reflection of how much control they have over other aspects of their lives—devotional habits, money, and use of time, to name a few. Can you choose to do what you know is right regardless of how you feel, or are you a slave to your urges? Can you defer gratification?

The need for self-control affects so many areas of our lives that the lack of it can render us virtually useless to the Lord. Paul said, "I beat my body and make it my slave so that after I have preached to others, I myself will not be disqualified for the prize" (1 Corinthians 9:27). Peter added, "For a man is slave to whatever has mastered him" (2 Peter 2:19).

As Christians, our lives are like a two-track model train; one track represents life in the Spirit, while the other represents life in the flesh. The train can't run on both tracks simultaneously. The question is, to which track will you throw the power switch *on*? When you choose to allow your spiritual drive to dominate and energize you, the desires of the flesh go dormant. Your train will run in the power of the Spirit, exhibiting the Spirit's fruit—self-control. Moment by moment, you must decide which track will have the power.

Whichever drive you feed the most will control you. If you know that certain friends, books, records, activites, or manners of dress energize your physical drive, steer clear of those influences. If you acknowledge that the Word and genuine Christian fellowship activate the power of the Spirit, then cultivate those habits and watch self-control take root and bloom afresh.

Sexual Fasting

Is it possible to be in control of your sexual desires, living in purity, but experience no struggles? John White, in *Eros Defiled*, refers to such a state as "sexual fasting," and compares it to abstinence from food.

> Starving people can be in one of two states. Some experience hunger as torture. They fight, steal, even kill to get food. Others experience no hunger at all.
>
> It depends upon the attitude (or mindset) of the starving person. If, for instance, I decide voluntarily to fast, I will experience hunger for a couple of days and then suddenly a strange absence of hunger. If, on the other hand, I have no wish to fast and you deprive me of food, I will spend my

days drooling over visions of it and my nights dreaming about it. My hunger will grow intolerable.[1]

Similarly, there can be an absence of turmoil—complete peace—for the single person who decides to fast from sensual pleasure, while his double-minded brother or sister experiences defeat. The crucial factor is one's mindset.

What happens to all that unused sexual energy? It is rechanneled as creative energy in other areas of our lives. Our sexual energy is *sublimated*. As defined by Webster, the word *sublimate* means "to divert the expression of (an instinctual desire or impulse) from its primitive form to one that is considered more socially or culturally acceptable."[2] God sublimates your normal sexual appetite, producing new impetus and creativity in other areas.

The principle of sublimation has long been accepted on a larger societal scale. J. D. Unwin, a respected Cambridge University sociologist, found in his study of over eighty ancient, primitive, and more modern societies that there was an unvarying correlation between the degree of sexual restraints and the rate of social progress. "Cultures that were more sexually permissive displayed less cultural energy, creativity, intellectual development, individualism, and a slower general cultural ascent."[3]

Arnold Toynbee, the renowned student of world history, believed that a culture that postpones sexual experience in young adults is more prone to progress. In their lifelong research project, *The Story of Civilization*, the late Will and Ariel Durant declare that sex in the young "is a river of fire that must be banked and cooled by a hundred restraints if it is not to consume in chaos both the individual and the group."[4]

Dating with a Mindset of Purity

Rosalie de Rosset writes,

> There is little praise for the consistently sexually controlled
> single. Too often, it is mixed with granulated pity or
> powdered condescension. Ironically, while discipline and
> self-control are encouraged and admired in scholarship,
> athletics, music and ministry, their absence is strangely ex-
> cused in sexual matters. The secular myth has infiltrated
> the Christian consciousness: our sexual urges are over-
> powering and irresistible. There will come the moment
> when we "simply can't help ourselves," when "madness"
> will overtake us, when "it will be bigger than us." To resist
> the madness is somehow a failure to comprehend true sex-
> uality, to be pronounced neuter—if not audibly, then cer-
> tainly subconsciously.[5]

It's easy for Christians to question whether victory in
the area of sexual purity is really possible in a culture as
overstimulated as ours. But consider for a moment the
first-century Corinthian society at the time the gospel was
introduced. Corinth was the sensual Disneyland of its day,
the center for the worship of Aphrodite, the goddess of fer-
tility. Young people were subject to conscription as temple
prostitutes. This hedonistic culture joined two of man's
strongest desires, worship and sex, into one perverted act.

Knowing this should give real power to the thirteenth
verse of 1 Corinthians 10: "No temptation has seized you
except what is common to man. And God is faithful; he
will not let you be tempted beyond what you can bear. But
when you are tempted, he will also provide a way out so
that you can stand up under it." If God could promise vic-

tory and deliverance for these people, surely he can do as much for us.

The Bible tells us that what was written to people in earlier times was "written to teach us, so that through endurance and the encouragement of the Scriptures we might have hope" (Romans 15:4). Any hope for a pure thought life rests on regular intake of the word.

Picture your life as a hilltop on which rain falls. As the water drains off, rivulets, representing the sensual habit patterns of our lives, form. Eventually some rivulets become swollen creeks. Saturating our minds with God's word allows him to control the flow of water. Slowly, but none the less dramatically, he uses his word to redirect the rivulets of our lives.

Tim LaHaye states that, "mental adultery has probably brought more sincere men to spiritual defeat than any other single sin."[6] Since lust is a private sin, it seems acceptable to permit sensual mental daydreams. But it's Satan's clever tactic to gain a foothold in your thought life that later gives birth to sin that's not so private. Satan is out to destroy you, and his favorite battleground is your mind. We must clothe ourselves "with the Lord Jesus Christ, and . . . not think about how to gratify the desires of the sinful nature" (Romans 13:14).

Victory over lust can be summarized in three words: *Resist the beginnings.* As 2 Corinthians 10:5 says, "Take captive every thought to make it obedient to Christ." Let that first hint of temptation be a springboard to prayer: "Thanks, Lord, that you've given me normal, healthy physical desires. But help me to turn from dwelling on this to dwelling on you."

Do we mean that one day you can hope to awaken and

be totally and forever free of impure thoughts and tugging sensual desires? God usually does not remove the physical longing." Victory is tenuous, but not impossible. The question to ask yourself is, Am I making progress?

Notice that the admonition to "flee the evil desires of youth" is followed by "and pursue righteousness, faith, love and peace" (2 Timothy 2:22). God does not give us a command in a vacuum; it's not just that we turn away *from* sin, but also that we turn *to* a positive replacement. As we fill our minds and our days with his priorities, we lessen our chances for succumbing to ever-present sexual temptations around us.

Dating with a Lifestyle of Purity

A person who keeps high standards of purity is sometimes an anachronism, even in Christian circles. A friend of ours was excited when a guy in her Sunday school class asked her out. They went out a half dozen times, but when Marnie told him that she wanted to keep the relationship without physical contact, he never asked her out again. In a sense, Marnie felt it was better not to start the car than to have to put it in reverse. Let us illustrate her viewpoint.

Fruit salesmen frequent our neighborhood with fresh truckloads from California. But my wife is prudent. She knows that she can buy the same fruit cheaper in the grocery store.

On one occasion, however, it was a different story. Before Paula could get one word out, the salesman said, "*Taste* this orange." She consented and within five minutes she was following him down to his truck, checkbook in hand. Later I nonchalantly asked her why she happened to get so many oranges this week. She replied sheepishly, "Honey, I knew those weren't the best buy, but they tasted so good that I couldn't resist them."

The point is that in sexual matters, few of us have enough self-control to be able to taste sensual pleasure to any degree and turn back. Just like my wife, we find ourselves buying fruit we never intended to.

Getting Your Own Convictions
Perhaps you wish someone would spell out the limits of physical contact; for example, "If you hold her hand and give her one kiss on the top side of her cheekbone, you're okay. Beyond that is sin." Or, "As long as you stay above the jaw and below the knee, you're safe."

Maybe it would be easier if we could draw the line for you. But then, when the lights were turned low and the music soft, you could pitch out our opinion with little remorse. If you come to your own guidelines as personal, prayed-about convictions before God, your conscience can't be ignored as easily.

As Alice Fryling puts it, "In today's society the idea for a Christian is not to see how close to the edge you can get without falling off, but how circumspectly you can walk to avoid potential danger."[7] What pushes you toward that edge might be as simple as holding hands; for another, the turn-on might be more intimate. You must decide.

Theoretically, many people feel that any activity that falls short of actual intercourse is natural and to be expected in the course of dating. But such a presupposition ignores the way God made us.

First, our "sexual computers" are not programmed to

operate on a cycle of starting and stopping, starting and stopping. Physical intimacy is *meant* to continue to the resolution of intercourse. If you develop the habit of petting, not only will you allow the physical area of your relationship to dominate, but you may shortcircuit your ability to respond normally to sex in marriage. Your motor may stop when it should be in full gear.

Second, God did not intend for us to continually engage in physical intimacy that leaves us unsatisfied. Some call this the "domino theory of love." With each contact, your desire accelerates but the thrill of that particular activity decreases. In other words, if you really enjoyed kissing him last time, you're going to want more than that the next time.

Some Practical Pointers
Among Christians, dating is a contract. God makes us responsible for keeping his image on the life of another person untarnished. So far as we are able, we must preserve the other person's values and sense of dignity. This is the cornerstone principle upon which we build more specific suggestions.

Wayne Wright has wisely said, "The best companion against immorality is geography." This is not to suggest that you should move to the next state, but that if you plan ahead to avoid compromising situations and run from the ones you didn't plan ahead for, you won't be caught repeating the words of Bert and Ginny: "We just never thought that this would happen to us." Set your standards ahead of time, and then *talk about them*, if you suspect there might be any misunderstanding between you and your date. You'll add a great deal of freedom to the relationship and spare each other many stilted and awkward moments.

One particular situation to steer clear of is spending time together alone in an apartment or dorm room. You may have the purest of intentions initially, but the situation of two people alone in a bedroom encourages the worst. Many couples who never planned to become "involved" will attest to the fact that this basic principle was the one they foolishly circumvented.

Place a high premium on activity and conversation. Author John Powell has written, "The success or failure of human relationships is determined mainly by success or failure at communication."[8] God is in no way depriving you by placing the physical aspect of your relationships on "hold." He's allowing you the freedom to develop the art you'll spend most of your lifetime refining—communication.

Finally, let this verse be the motto for your date life: "Whatever you do, do it all for the glory of God" (1 Corinthians 10:31). If you go to a movie, let it be one that stimulates your mind, so that you'll be more discerning, *for his glory*. If you play Ping-Pong and pop popcorn, enjoy it to the fullest, that you might return rested and enthusiastic to what he's called you to, *for his glory*. If the time together leaves you enriched, encouraged, relaxed, stimulated; if it brings glory to the Lord, then you know it is time well spent.

Begin Now with a Clean Slate

A recent report published by the Alan Guttmacher Institute reveals that the average age for a guy's or girl's first sexual experience, is sixteen. Only one fifth of the males and one third of the females have not had intercourse by age nineteen. If such is the case, then many, including Christians, will have to make a fresh start with the Lord. In some ways the Christian life does have impossible standards—right actions that spring from right thoughts. To some degree, whether by thought or action, we have all fallen short of God's prescription for a sexually chaste life.

Today there is a tendency to deal with a guilty conscience by trying to lessen or deny the validity of God's blueprint for sexual purity ("no one can live a pure sexual life in a world like this"). However, to lower or deny God's standards not only makes matters worse for our guilty conscience, but offends his holiness. God's intention is that we acknowledge his standards for our lives while seeking his forgiveness in Christ when we miss the mark.

For some, this may be the most important section in this book. If your background includes immorality, and you've not drunk deeply at the wellspring of God's forgiveness, your past will become a noose around your neck that threatens to strangle your spiritual life. Remember that Paul said to Timothy, "The goal of our instruction is love from a pure heart and a *good conscience* and a sincere faith" (1 Timothy 1:5, NASB).

No sin you have committed is beyond God's forgiveness. Three of the women mentioned in Christ's genealogy (Matthew 1:1–16) were involved in overt sin. They were socially unacceptable, yet God chose to include these women in the genealogy of our Lord. God is in the business of forgiving and transforming sinners, a group for which we all have a calling card.

"As far as the east is from the west, so far has he removed our transgressions from us" (Psalm 103:12). "I, even

I, am he who blots out your transgressions, for my own sake, and remembers your sins no more" (Isaiah 43:25). God's forgiveness is complete and irrevocable for any person who is in Christ.

Consider Hebrews 9:13-14.

> The blood of goats and bulls and the ashes of a heifer sprinkled on those who are ceremonially unclean sanctify them so that they are outwardly clean. *How much more*, then, will the blood of Christ, who through the eternal Spirit offered himself unblemished to God, cleanse our consciences from acts that lead to death, so that we may serve the living God!

If you refuse to accept the forgiveness of God, you are saying that the blood of Christ is not enough to cover your sin and somehow you must add your penance. It increases your sin not to gratefully accept the forgiveness Christ purchased.

If inability to feel forgiven for your past is a problem that plagues you, may we offer some steps suggested to us by a counselor who has helped many people find their way out of a maze of guilt.

Complete Repentance
Ask God to bring to your mind everything from your past that haunts you presently and has violated his principles and commands. Make a list of all that comes to your mind.

Take the time to pray about everything on your list, perhaps in this way: "Lord, I really want to turn from my past. I know I did the wrong thing and I want to be free from ever falling prey to these sins again. Father, thank you that the blood of Christ covers my sin, even these sins.

Thank you that I can be forever free of these entangle-ments."

As you tear up your list and throw it away, continue to thank God for the way that he has bought you back from your past.

> As obedient children, do not conform to the evil desires
> you had when you lived in ignorance. For you know that
> it was not with perishable things such as silver or gold that
> you were redeemed from the empty way of life handed
> down to your from your forefathers, but with the precious
> blood of Christ, a lamb without blemish or defect (1 Peter
> 1:14, 18–19).

Complete Immersion
In the next weeks and months immerse yourself in the doc-trine of God's love and grace and mercy. Soak your mind in the Scriptures through Bible study, Scripture memory, and meditation, picking out verses and passages that herald God's forgiveness and acceptance of you.

Complete Transparency
For many people, this last step is unnecessary if they have followed through completely with the first two steps. However, if you feel that Satan still plagues you with feel-ings of guilt you are unable to shake, then it would be helpful for you to open up your life to an older person who is more mature in the faith and able to accept and counsel you. This step is based on the Scriptural principle in James 5:16—"Therefore confess your sins to each other and pray for each other so that you may be healed." While transparency always involves risk, God sometimes uses another person to mirror his love and acceptance and

forgiveness back to us, and thereby heal the wounds of our past.

At some point, you must leave the past in the past, and move on. The apostle Paul was responsible for the persecution of many Christians, and he was a passive participant in the stoning of Stephen. Thus he speaks from painful experience when he writes, "Forgetting what is behind and straining toward what is ahead, I press on toward the goal to win the prize for which God has called me heavenward in Christ Jesus" (Philippians 3:13-14).

It remains for you to offer you body to God as a living and holy sacrifice, as an act of spiritual worship (Romans 12:1). God will take your misshapen lump of clay, redeemed by the blood of the perfect Lamb, and remake it into a vessel of honor. Your body and life maintained in the purity he intended can become a reflection of his personality, a credit to his glory.

Notes   1. John White, *Eros Defiled: The Christian and Sexual Sin* (InterVarsity Press, 1978), page 28.

2. *Webster's New Collegiate Dictionary* (G. & C. Merriam Company, 1974), page 1159.

3. J. D. Unwin, as quoted in "How to Put Premarital Sex on Hold," by Reo M. Christenson, *Christianity Today*, 19 February 1982, page 17.

4. Will and Ariel Durant, as quoted in "How to Put Premarital Sex on Hold."

5. Rosalie de Rosset, "Chaste by Choice," *Christianity Today*, 19 February 1982, page 18.

6. Tim LaHaye, *The Act of Marriage* (Zondervan, 1976), page 31.

7. "The Domino Theory of Dating," Alice Fryling, *His*, February 1975, page 16.

8. "Six Insights Which Changed John Powell," as quoted from his book, *Fully Human, Fully Alive* (Argus, 1976) in Idea-Source, edited by Monte Unger.

Questions for Study and Personal Application

1. God's will concerning our bodies is very clear for believers. Read 1 Thessalonians 4:3–8.
   a. What are we to do?
   b. What are we not to do?
   c. Based on God's will, what would the dating relationship be like between two Christians?

2. Read James 1:13–15. Describe the path to sin.

3. Based on Luke 6:45, how can we inventory our thoughts?

4. How do we go about changing our thought life? Look up the following verses and jot down some thoughts in answer to this question.
   a. Deuteronomy 6:6–7
   b. Joshua 1:8
   c. Psalm 119:9 and 11
   d. 2 Corinthians 10:5

5. What environments or activities can produce wrong thoughts in your mind? What should you do when that happens?

6. How would you personally define purity in a dating relationship? Be as specific as you think you need to be.

7. How does Proverbs 22:3 apply to the activities and locations of a date?

8. According to 1 John 1:9, what is our responsibility when we become aware of sin in our lives?

9. What does God do with our sin as Christians? Answer this question from the following verses.
   a. Psalm 103:12
   b. Isaiah 38:17
   c. Isaiah 43:25
   d. Micah 7:19

10. What is your present attitude toward pure dating relationships? In what way, if any, has this study encouraged you to change your attitudes and actions?

Scripture memory assignment: 1 Thessalonians 4:3

Special project: Write down what your standards in the physical area of dating will be from now on.

Questions for Discussion

Question 1: What does it mean to defraud someone? What are some ways that men defraud women in a dating relationship? What are some ways that women defraud men? What percentage of your friends, Christian and non-Christian, have immoral physical relationships outside of marriage? What are some reasons why this is so?

Question 4: Can you share an illustration of how God changed your thoughts through Scripture memorization and meditation?

Question 5: How can a person's thought life affect his actions in a dating relationship?

Question 6: Why should Christians pursue purity in dating?

Question 7: For two Christians committed to purity in dating, what are some activites and circumstances to avoid?

Question 9: Can you share what effect the truth of God's forgiveness has had on your life?

8
Singleness

MY SON, BRADY, and I play a game called "Mine." No doubt you've played it, too, if you've been around small children. It goes like this: I grab an object and say, "Mine. This belongs to me." Then Brady laughs and snatches the object from my hand. Clutching it to his chest, he says, "No, mine." Back and forth we go with this scenario until one of us tires. Then I grab Brady and hug him. "Brady, you're mine. You belong to me." His face absolutely radiates the sheer pleasure of being wanted, of *belonging* to someone.

Brady is reflecting, with childlike transparency, what we all feel—the need to belong to someone, to be sought after, to be wanted. We tend to think this need can best be met in a dating relationship, and later in marriage. As we get caught in the wheels of a world seemingly geared for couples, our need to belong to another person intensifies.

What an incredible thought to realize that we *belong* to God. We have been purchased from every tribe and tongue and people and nation with the expensive blood of his Son. We are his. All other shades of belonging pale in comparison. My husband will die, and my children don't really belong to me. No human relationship can supplant or overshadow the joy of knowing *whose* I am.

As you consider the question of dating and marriage, you must be sure that you aren't seeking a relationship with someone as a substitute for basking in belonging to Christ. You are complete in him. Grasping your completeness, your wholeness in Christ, frees you to consider the single life as a viable option, one that might be the good and perfect and acceptable will of God for you.

Marriage Could Be Second Best

The apostle Paul considered the single life the best way to live. To those of us who have spent any time looking wistfully over the fence of our single state into the pasture of presumed marital bliss, we find that attitude hard to comprehend. However, Paul's reasons for applauding the advantages of the single life remain as unassailable today as when he penned them. It's altogether plausible that marriage could be second best.

> Because of the present crisis, I think that it is good for you to remain as you are. Are you married? Do not seek a

divorce. Are you unmarried? Do not look for a wife. But if you do marry, you have not sinned; and if a virgin marries, she has not sinned. But those who marry will face many troubles in this life, and I want to spare you this. What I mean, brothers, is that the time is short. From now on those who have wives should live as if they had none . . . I would like you to be free from concern. (1 Corinthians 7:26–32)

In View of the Present Crisis

Few of us would argue that our world is in a crisis. These are perilous, unstable, demanding times in which we live. As Christians we're caught in a paradox: Though we are destined for the world to come, we must live as salt—a preservative—in this present world.

As our culture declines, we can expect the hostility of the world around us to increase, not lessen. At any point at which salt touches the sores of the world, the potential for healing arises, but not without excruciating pain in the process. If you marry and have children, then you must contend with opposition not only toward yourself, but toward those closest to you as well. Scripture says, "because of the present crisis" you will face less turmoil and hostility from the world if you remain single.

In View of a Simpler Life

When we say that a single's life is simpler, eyebrows inevitably rise. After all, many singles have lawns to mow, income tax forms to fill out, cars to buy, and moving boxes to unpack. The assertion that a single person's life is simpler refers mainly to the network of relationships with which he has to deal.

If you consider the average family with two adults and two children, there are only four people, but actually twelve existing relationships (husband to wife, father to son, brother to sister, and so on)—all of which need to run smoothly. This affects many aspects of daily life. For example, when a single person decides to buy a car, he usually has only his needs and desires to take into acount. A family, however, may invest hours in the discussion of that same purchase. There are more people and more factors to take into consideration. Marriage also introduces a person into a web of relationships (the extended families of each partner) that can be a tremendous blessing or a time-consuming headache at given points.

In the *King James Version*, 1 Corinthians 7:28 reads, "Nevertheless such shall have trouble in the flesh." Pastor John MacArthur points out that the word *flesh* refers to our lower nature, and the word *trouble* is derived from a Greek word meaning "to press together."[1] In marriage, your humanness presses against that of your partner. Conflicts result, as they inevitably do in any close relationship. Are you willing to invest an evening deciding whose home you'll visit for Christmas or whether you'll spend your income tax money on a camper or a computer? Can you adjust to decisions you disagree with? Such is the reality of daily life on the marital side of the fence.

It could be pointed out, and rightly so, that this is one purpose for which God designed marriage—to smooth some of the rough spots in our character as we rub against another person. Marriage can act as a curb on selfishness and inflexibility. Be that as it may, the truth remains that a single person goes through life with fewer restraints and complications.

In View of Your Availability for God

At no other time in history has the goal of taking the gospel to every living creature been so within our reach. But now as in the annals of church history, these words echo: "I have taken a wife and cannot come." Paul is not saying that it is *wrong* to marry, but he would have you consider the possibility that God might use you uniquely as a single person. He says in verse thirty-two of 1 Corinthians 7, "I would like you to be free from concern." The Greek more literally translates "free from concern" as "without trouble," conveying the idea of not being weighed down with the cares of the world. In a special way, the single person is free to concentrate his time and energy on spiritual things. His effort and attention can remain undivided.

Paul says emphatically in this passage, "Be a realist." Consider what you want to give the bulk of your time to. It's not unspiritual to spend hours assessing the best buy in a second car or deciding whether the children have sufficient winter clothes; this is just the way married life is.

In verse thirty-five, Paul gives the foundational advantage for the single life: "that you may live in a right way in undivided devotion to the Lord." How would you describe undivided devotion? Here is an example in a young Communist's letter to his girlfriend explaining why he can no longer continue the relationship.

> There is one thing in which I am dead earnest about and that is the communist cause. It is my life, my business, my religion. It is my hobby, my sweetheart, my wife, my mistress, my bread, my meat. I work at it in the daytime and I dream of it at night. Its hold on me grows, not lessens, as time goes on. Therefore, I cannot carry on a relationship

with you any longer, no longer a love affair, not even a conversation with others without relating it to this force which drives and guides my life. I evaluate books and people and ideas and actions according to how they affect this communist cause and by their attitude toward it. I've already been in jail because of my ideals, and, if necessary, I'm ready to go before a firing squad.[2]

This is not the prototype for every Christian single's lifestyle, but it demonstrates what it means to be wholeheartedly giving yourself to a cause, albeit the wrong one.

Consider Whether Before You Consider Who

It is only fitting that you entertain the question of remaining single as you consider dating and marriage from God's perspective. In fact, many would say that a willingness to remain single for Christ's sake is prerequisite to readiness for marriage in Christ to the right person. It is similar to other decisions of the Christian life. While I might prefer to live within a few hundred miles of the mountains where I grew up, I must be willing—really willing—to live at the equator for Christ's sake. Otherwise I won't be free to enjoy the geography he places me in. We simply cannot dictate to God the terms under which we will serve him.

How many countless hours have been spent agonizing over the question, Do I have the gift of singleness? Elisabeth Elliot says, "What we are is a gift, and, like other gifts, chosen by the giver alone. We are not presented with an array of options."[3] In other words, consider your singleness in the same light others consider marriage: both are gifts of God, given as a mark of his goodness. God has not left you to worry over whether the gift of singleness is yours for a lifetime. The grace to live contentedly in this state or any other is yours for today.

Make the Most of Singleness

How then do you deal with the ramifications and feelings of being a single person in day-to-day life? Both singleness and marriage have particular limitations, as well as compensations. But the world can make life particularly difficult for the person who is insecure with his singleness. As one guy said, "I grew to feel as though there was something wrong with me; I didn't have what it takes—I was defective merchandise. My thinking changed and I relaxed as I saw that God might be trying to bless me with what I previously saw as a curse."

Your response to the following aspects of life will determine whether being single is a blessing or a curse for you.

What You Think of Yourself
How you live is determined by your self-concept. From the moment you enter the Christian life until you actually stand before God's presence, one of the major ministries of the Holy Spirit is to affirm your identity in Christ and your worth before a holy, loving Father.

It is the plan of Satan to convince you that you are unworthy: "You're no good. You'll never be any different—always hung up with the same problems." At those times, remember A. W. Tozer's advice.

If the devil does come to you and whispers that you are no good, don't argue with him. In fact, you may as well admit it, but then remind the devil: "Regardless of what you say about me, I must tell you how the Lord feels about me. He tells me that I am so valuable to Him that He gave Himself for me on the cross. So, the value is set by the price paid—and, in our case, the price paid was our Lord himself!"[4]

Our worth before God is determined by the immeasurable value of his Son.

The inablility to grasp our worth in God's eyes and to develop a positive self-image is shared by many people, single or not. Ever since the Fall, man has been confused over who he is and who God is. If the problem of a low self-image is a recurring one for you, keep in mind there are no quick solutions. You may know in your mind that you were chosen before the foundation of the world, were bought with a high price, and are precious to God. But transferring that knowledge from your head to your heart is a more difficult matter. You may think, "I wouldn't be feeling this way again if I were doing the right thing. There must be some solution to this I haven't tried; something that will give me a permanent 'I-feel-good-about-myself' attitude."

The habit of meditating on God's opinion of you as stated plainly in his word, and thanking God repeatedly for the way he made you (even the things you don't like), is indispensable. It's like treating a serious burn on your leg. Healing will come in time with the repeated, diligent application of a basic remedy.

You cannot migrate from a negative self-image to a healthy, posiƟve one with a single cursory application of

God's essential truths. Only by inhaling, faithfully and consistently, the fresh breeze of your worth before God will you expel the stale, pungent odor of inferiority and inadequacy.

How You Treat Yourself

Your appearance, the way you fix your room, apartment, or house, and the friends you have often reveal more to others than you realize. What kind of message are you communicating to them? If a stranger came to your door, would he know that place was home to you, or wonder if you were just passing through? Would he notice your attire and wonder what you thought of yourself?

These may seem like unimportant details to you, but they are details of uncommon interest to the Lord, for they reveal your mind-set toward God's will for your life at the moment. It's important, for instance, that you emotionally move into the place in which you live. Your home should be decorated so that is reflects your personality and your tastes. Get out the things in your hope chest, so to speak, and enjoy them today.

Warm, supportive relationships with the opposite sex and with married people are sometimes hard to come by, but nevertheless invaluable, as are friendships with people of the same sex. One single friend remarked, "I place an especially high price tag on friendships with married couples. Watching their lives gives me a more realistic view of marriage and dispels my marriage myths." Whatever initiative it requires to feel a part of a caring group of Christians is worth all the effort.

God does not redeem us from our past failures and our future punishment and in between leave us to fend for ourselves. He wants to permeate every cubbyhole of our lives—our hobbies, our friendships, the music we listen to, the way we dress—until they all bear the mark of his grace.

What You Are Becoming

God is interested in you as a whole person, not just the part of you that might become a wife or husband, mother or father. Whether you marry or not, you're going to have to live with the person you are for a long time.

God is committed to conforming our character to the image of Christ. "And we, who with unveiled faces all reflect the Lord's glory, are being transformed into his likeness with ever-increasing glory" (2 Corinthians 3:18). God only asks for our pliability and cooperation. It's not so much that he demands perfection of us, but that he desires progress. C. S. Lewis once said, "God loves us in spite of our infirmities but He never ceases to will the removal of our imperfections."

Given such a premise, that the Lord wants to build godly character into our lives, many people falsely assume that when they reach an undefinable goal of spiritual maturity, he will bring along the right marriage partner. One twenty-six-year-old woman related, "I thought that if I embarked on a spiritual improvement program, God would then bring my husband into my life. I just needed to get ready." And so she set out to become a spiritual giant, a woman of God's word, an industrious, submissive counterpart for the right man who would walk into her life. When no man stepped into the picture, she felt shortchanged, let down, not good enough.

Marriage and spiritual maturity do not always accompany one another. A husband or wife is a gift from God, given or not given according to his perfect wisdom. Judy Douglas, author of *Old Maid Is a Dirty Word*, writes that "we are married or unmarried because it is God's will—not because we have made x number of spiritual points."[5] Marriage is not a spiritual merit badge to be earned.

Commit yourself, then, to becoming the person God wants you to be, single or married: "mature and complete, not lacking anything" (James 1:4). God desires to ingrain his image in the wood of your character, not so much to prepare you for a partner, as to prepare you for *life*. Your ultimate good and his glory are his primary concerns.

Waiting on the Lord

Not long ago we got into our car to go visit another family. For some reason our daughter, Allison, decided that the only acceptable place in which to make that trip was on my lap. Stacy thought otherwise, and placed her in the back seat behind me. She cried and whined and complained as though she had been perched on top of an antennae. "Allison," I tried to console her, "don't you realize we're just going around the corner?" As a child, what she perceived to be a marathon ride was only a two-block drive.

As adults we sometimes behave in the same childish way. We are quick to assume that we will live in a single state a few years longer than we might have chosen, or perhaps even a lifetime. And even though our singleness may be only a "two-block drive," it can become lonely, frustrating, and patience-stretching at times. Judy Douglas points out one temptation peculiarly suited to the single state, that of living for the future. "We view our jobs as temporary until a man (or woman) comes along. We remember wistfully or we dream hopefully, but we despair of the present, for there is no man (or woman) in the present."[6]

The Psalmist reminds us, "This is the day the Lord has made; let us rejoice and be glad in it" (Psalm 118:24). Today is the day to enter wholeheartedly into whatever the business is at hand. Don't wait in the wings for marriage to sound the cue that your act is on.

An important question to ask yourself is this: Am I happy in the Lord now? Is my relationship with him growing increasingly satisfying? If it is, don't worry for the future. At thirty-five or forty-five or sixty-five, whether you are in prison, on a yacht on the Caribbean, widowed, or childless, you will be content if your focus is on him, as David's was: "I have set the Lord always before me. Because he is at my right hand, I will not be shaken" (Psalm 16:8).

It would be a relief if this issue of contentment were a question that, once dealt with, never came to mind again. But it's not. Most singles acknowledge seasons of life in which waves of desire to be married, to experience human companionship, sweep over them with titanic force. With each recurrence you must choose either to coddle the yearning or to turn to God. If you allow your feelings to master you, that desire can grow to idolatrous proportions.

But if you come honestly to the Lord, as the Psalmist did, and admit, "All my longings lie open before you, O Lord; my sighing is not hidden from you" (Psalm 38:9), then he can reach down into your heart and give you added grace. One woman wisely said, "As I use such times to draw closer to the Lord, I've realized that I know aspects of God that the average married woman does not know. I know him as my Best Friend, my Helper, my Choicest Companion—needs that the Lord commonly meets for a married woman through her husband." The lonely times become an invitation to get closer to him, remembering that the Lord himself, often misunderstood and rejected, was single for thirty-three years. "For we do not have a high priest who is unable to sympathize with our weaknesses" (Hebrews 4:15).

I asked a close friend who was single until she was thirty-seven what helped her the most when she experienced a period of discontent and desire to be married. "Every morning," she explained, "when I first awakened, I thanked the Lord that by his grace and his plan I was single at this point, doing what he wanted me to do. Acknowledging that God's perfect plan for me was in force each day brought me to a place of acceptance. As I was faithful to apply the balm of thanksgiving, God lifted me out of every low period that came along." As John White asks in *Eros Defiled*, "Would you despise intimacy with the Almighty in insisting on more of human intimacy?"[7]

Notes   1. John MacArthur, "Singleness as a Gift of the Spirit," *Moody Monthly*, January 1977, pages 89-90.

2. As quoted in *Singleness*, by Charles R. Swindoll (Multnomah Press, 1981), page 22.

3. Elisabeth Elliot, *Let Me Be a Woman* (Tyndale House Publishers, 1976), page 33.

4. A. W. Tozer, *The Best of A. W. Tozer*, compiled by Warren W. Wiersbe (Baker Book House, 1978), page 227.

5. Judy Douglas, *Old Maid Is a Dirty Word* (Here's Life Publishers, 1979), page 42.

6. Douglas, page 54.

7. John White, *Eros Defiled: The Christian and Sexual Sin* (InterVarsity Press, 1977), page 138.

Questions for Personal Study and Application

1. How do the following verses relate to singleness: Psalm 73:25-26; Jeremiah 29:11; 1 Timothy 6:6?

2. Look up Psalm 139:13-14; Matthew 11:28-29; Luke 12:7; and Romans 9:20. What thoughts do you have about God's concern for you and control of your circumstances?

3. Read 1 Corinthians 7:25-35.
   a. What are Paul's reasons for encouraging the single life?
   b. Paraphrase verses twenty-six and thirty-two.

4. As given in 1 Corinthians 7:1-10, what are some reasons to get married, and what are some reasons to remain single?

5. Read Matthew 19:3-12.
   a. Why did the disciples think it might be better not to marry?
   b. What three reasons for celibacy does Jesus give?

6. Do you think it is possible to live a fulfilled life as a single person? Why or why not?

7. Review the previous questions and list both the pros and cons for a life of celibacy. Then add some of your own reasons for and against marriage.

Scripture memory assignment: 1 Corinthians 7:7

Special project: Spend time with the Lord, honestly examining your attitude toward your gift of singleness.

Questions for Discussion

Question 1: What are the lifestyles of some of your Christian acquaintances over thirty who have not yet been married? In what ways do you see application of these verses—or the lack of it—in the attitudes and actions of these people?

Question 2: What are some of culture's pressures against not yet being married or planning to remain single? How can the verses listed be helpful in withstanding those pressures?

Question 3: How would you describe "undivided devotion"? Do you know someone who has made a decision to remain single for this purpose? What is his or her life like?

Question 4: What do you think Paul meant in verse seven?

Question 5: What do you think Jesus meant in verse eleven?

Question 6: How does your view of your marital status affect the way you view God's plans for your life?

9

This Is Getting Serious

FOR A NUMBER of years my wife and I have approached our single friends with what we consider to be an unbeatable proposition. For a small fee, we will send out their resumé of marriageable traits, background, and preferences, and then interview prospective marriage partners who reply. We back our services with a two-year warranty: "Results guaranteed, or your money courteously refunded." Strangely enough, not one person has taken us up on this offer. In this day and culture, no one wants to settle the question of mate selection by proxy!

Once you have considered whether or not you want to marry, and have decided that you are open to the possibility of marriage, you must deal with the question of who is the right person. Who do you want to spend a lifetime getting to know? Whose curlers can you endure? Whose soggy, wadded-up washcloth do you want to hang up daily? Whose weaknesses are you willing to tolerate, and whose joys and sorrows are you anxious to share?

Wouldn't it be convenient if we could settle this question with the same confidence that Abraham's servant had as he set out to find a bride for Isaac? "Oh Lord . . . may it be that when I say to a girl, 'Please let down your jar that I may have a drink,' and she says, 'Drink, and I'll water your camels too'—let her be the one you have chosen for your servant Isaac" (Genesis 24:12–14). When a lovely girl named Rebekah responded in such a fashion, Abraham's servant knew his mission was accomplished.

Can you see this scene reenacted in a twentieth century rendition? "Oh Lord, let the first girl who offers me a Coke before nine o'clock be the one for me." Sounds ridiculous, doesn't it? Hopefully, your approach to choosing a mate will be more realistic and mature.

How Will You Recognize Real Love?

Possibly you are wondering as you read this book whether a current dating relationship, or perhaps a past one, constitutes real love and is a relationship you should pursue. You want to know, and rightly so, whether or not the twitchiness in your stomach is indicative of a love that endures or just starry-eyed infatuation. As you reflect on this, consider the differences between real love and what *seems* to be love

Real Love Is Knowledgeable

If what you are feeling for another person is love, then that feeling will be based on having seen the other person in many situations over a period of time. Love deepens as knowledge of the other person grows and many aspects of his or her personality attract you. Ask yourself, How many characteristics of this person can I list, and what proof do I have to substantiate those traits?

On the other hand, if what you're feeling is infatuation, the number of factors that attract you to him or her is relatively few. You're bewitched by her blue eyes or enamored of his athletic ability, but how about his or her lifestyle and goals? Is it an affinity for pizza and movies that binds you together, or a shared outlook on life?

When two people are infatuated, they live in a romantic Fantasyland. Whether they've known each other for a few months or even a number of years, faults and weaknesses are hidden behind a superficial guise. Each person loves the image he or she has created of the other.

Dr. James Peterson summarizes the characteristics of infatuated love (which he refers to as romance).

> First, romance results in such distortions of personality that after marriage the two people can never fulfill the roles that they expect of the other. Second, romance so idealizes marriage and even sex that when the day-to-day experiences of marriage are encountered there, must be disillusionment involved. Third, the romantic complex is so shortsighted that the premarital relationship is conducted almost entirely on the emotional level and consequently, such problems as temperamental or value differences, religious or cultural differences, financial, occupational,

or health problems are never considered. Fourth, romance develops such a false ecstasy that there is implied in courtship promise of a kind of happiness which could never be maintained during the realities of married life. Fifth, romance is such an escape from the negative aspects of personality to the extent that their repression obscures the real person.[1]

A person who experiences real love is not afraid to admit his own shortcomings, or those of the other person. Could you say, "I am fully aware of your temper, and I love you in spite of your short fuse"? While it is true that you usually have a somewhat idealized conception of the person you love, nevertheless there must be a total willingness to check that perception with reality and accept what you see.

The foundation of love upon which you build a lifetime relationship must be knowledgeable, unconditional commitment to the one you marry. As Maxine Hancock writes, "It's knowing that you and she will still care about each other when sex and day dreams, fights, and futures—when all that's on the shelf and done with. Love—well I'll tell you what love is: It's you at seventy-five and her at seventy-one, each of you listening for the other's step in the next room, each afraid that sudden silence, a sudden cry, could mean a lifetime's talk is over."[2]

Real Love Is a Response to the Total Person
Of the three Greek words for love—*eros*, *phileō*, and *agapē*—infatuation consists almost exclusively of the first two, eros and phileō. Eros is a sensual, sexual expression of love that seeks to enjoy and possess the object of affection.

The response is more to a body and a face than a total person, complete with mind, emotions and personality. If the element of physical communication is removed from the relationship, there is often little attraction left. It is commonly associated with the phrase, "I love you if" (you do such and such to please me).

Phileō is that variety of rapport we call "brotherly love," a type of mutual appreciation where both people benefit from a relationship of shared interests. "I love you because" (of some particular trait) is the phrase often used to illustrate phileō love.

Agapē love is an unconditional response to the total person: "I love you in spite of" (the weaknesses I see in you). Any relationship that endures must possess this level of concern for the welfare of someone without any desire to control that person, to be thanked by him, or to enjoy the process. It reaches beyond to a "willingness to give when the loved one is not able to reciprocate, whether it be because of illness, failure, or simply an hour of weakness. It is a love that can repair bonds severed by unfaithfulness, indifference, or jealousy."[3] The best example of this type of love is God himself. "For God so loved the world that he *gave*" (John 3:16).

Many people who are happily married readily admit that they were attracted to their future husband or wife's personality and character long before they were fully aware of an appealing appearance. "I didn't notice he was such a nice looking guy at first," is a comment you often hear from couples whose relationships have thrived upon many shared interests. Their physical attraction to one another was supported by a lasting foundation of friendship and respect.

Real Love Edifies

We had known Jim and Leslie as single people for years and had seen their relationships with God develop and their personalities unfold. What we were amazed to observe, though, were the incredibly positive personality traits that surfaced in them as individuals as the result of their love for each other. Everyone who knew them well remarked on the differences. Leslie arrived places on time. Jim exhibited more sensitivity to people around him. And both were more self-confident and assured as individuals. No one should have been surprised, though, because real love produces positive, constructive changes in an individual.

But how many times have you heard comments like these: "I'm not surprised that Sandra forgot her dentist appointment today. She's in another world. Nothing else matters but spending time with Joe." Sandra is probably infatuated with Joe, and the chances are good that in a few months, Sandra will be "gone" over someone else.

We commonly expect someone "in love" to be irresponsible, living in a one-person world. Movies and soap operas support such assumptions. "Joe is my reason for living" is the spoken or unspoken thought conveyed. But when the fog clears, the reality dawns—if Joe is your reason for living, you haven't got much of a reason.

When a couple is really in love, their relationship becomes a plus, not a replacement for other people and activities. Their love is secure enough to survive separation and mature enough to accept the responsibilities as well as the pleasures of the relationship.

Infatuated love, however, insists upon continual reassurance from the other person. It makes unreasonable demands that stem from possessiveness and insecurity.

Charted on graph paper, it would range from high peaks of certainty to valleys of doubt. Unstable in its duration, infatuation is like a seasonal monsoon; it comes, blows fiercely, and moves on.

Ask Yourself These Questions

As you consider whether the flutters you're feeling are love, the kind that would prompt you to leave your present home and begin a new one, take careful stock of the quality of your love. Are you willing to wait for the fulfillment of that love as Jacob did? He "served seven years to get Rachel, but they seemed like only a few days to him because of his love for her" (Genesis 29:20).

Can you honestly say that you are willing and able to put that person's needs and desires ahead of your own? Is his or her happiness uppermost in your thinking? Hermann Oeser, a German author, writes, "Those who want to become happy should not marry. The important thing is to make the other one happy. Those who want to be understood should not marry. The important thing is to understand one's partner."[4]

Could your love thrive without physical expression? If your spouse had an accident that maimed or disfigured him or her for life, could you still care? Such are some of the questions and considerations you must weigh if you would accurately assess the quality of your love.

Is There Only One Right Person?

Chuck Swindoll believes that "success in life consists not so much in marrying the person who will make you happy as in escaping the many who could make you miserable."[5]

uch words are fundamentally true, but they imply that there is only one right marriage partner for each of us. Many arduous, needle-in-the-haystack searches have taken place for that one right person, partly because we long to hear it said of our love relationship, "Aren't they the perfect match?"

If such is the case, that we could only be happy with one person, then how does one explain the happy marriages in this world that are arranged by the parents? What about the man whose first wife dies, and who, after his remarriage to another woman, openly admits that he loves both women?

Could it be more realistic to say that one should marry *a* right person rather than *the* right person?

Obviously we're caught in a tension of truths. God is in control, as Job said: "I know that you can do all things; no plan of yours can be thwarted" (Job 42:2). Yet it is equally true that God gives us the freedom to make wise choices within his prescribed moral limits. The Bible says a Christian can only marry another believer, which in one sense is very limiting (it discounts much of the world), and in another sense is very broad (there are many Christians). From within the body of Christians, then, we must make a spiritually wise choice. We can't ignore either God's sovereignty or our responsibility.

Before marriage, you must be concerned with making a wise, knowledgeable decision in the choice of a marriage partner. That is the time to wrestle with making a "right" choice; after marriage you'll labor to make that decision "right."

Let me say that another way. Before I married Paula, I

spent hours getting to know her and hours apart from her, seeking the Lord and getting some counsel from people who knew us well. I struggled to make a wise decision before God. Now I give myself wholeheartedly to making our marriage work.

Make a Wise Choice

Paula and I love to do premarital counseling. The first thing we do when a couple comes to us is ask them to make a list of every reason why they want to marry the person sitting with them. Those lists are fascinating. We've heard some as detailed and thorough as a salesman's description of a Mercedes, and some as simple as "I love Sue and she loves me."

Simply put, "I love you" is not enough. It's an inadequate reason to marry. Certainly you should feel that you are in love with the person you're going to marry, that you are exhilarated in his or her presence and keenly aware of his or her absence. But there must be an objective basis to those feelings. *Balance* is the ultimate goal.

SUBJECTIVE (WHAT DO I FEEL?)	OBJECTIVE (DO I HAVE A BASIS FOR THIS FEELING?)

The Greeks said it best—"Emotion must warm reason, but reason must rule emotion."[6] The reason that balances emotion should come from the meshing of your backgrounds, values, and personalities.

Background

We filter the people around us through our background, almost subconsciously pursuing or rejecting relationships on the basis of racial, ethnic, socio-economic, and educational similarites or differences. (Although people who have opposite temperaments are often attracted to each other, social opposites seldom are.)

Most people admit that only after they get married and establish a home of their own do they see how much their backgrounds come into play. They affect everything from how you celebrate holidays to whether you spend money on books or sirloin steaks. This is not to say that a high school graduate can never expect to be happily married to someone with a Ph.D., or that a marriage of a Korean and an American won't work. But the differences must be faced squarely ahead of time.

While it is true that in Christ "there is no Greek and Jew, circumcised or uncircumcised, barbarian, Scythian, slave or free" (Colossians 3:11), yet the fact remains that people with similar backgrounds have fewer points that rub against each other, and thus fewer adjustments.

Values

The values, goals, and outlook on life of two people in a relationship call for active, thoughtful discernment. As stated before in chapter five, the factor about which there can be no compromise is the question of commitment to Christ.

I am continually amazed at how often Christians ignore the clear teaching of the Scriptures. Recently I was with a group of Christians and observed the enthusiasm and hunger to grow of one girl in particular. Later I learned that she was newly married to a man who was not a Christian and had absolutely no observable spiritual interest. "How did this happen?" I asked.

It seems that when an older woman described in church one day how her husband had become a Christian after they married, the younger woman took this as a sign from the Lord that he would bless her own union to a non-Christian. The problem is that no matter how strongly you feel or how conclusive the circumstantial "signs" may be, you can never make a decision that is contrary to clear Scriptural teaching and be within the will of God. His will never violates his word.

Once you know that a person is a Christian however, the question arises of how deep that commitment is. If you could draw a picture of the commitment of a person you are dating, what diagram would it look like?

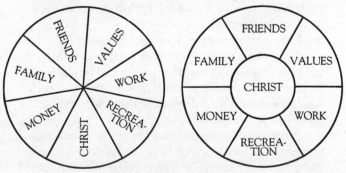

Is Christ the center of his or her life? Does Christ permeate every facet, or is he merely present as a "slice of the pie," just another activity or interest?

Sometimes two committed Christians who are strongly attracted to each other make the faulty assumption that "obviously, we should get married." Perhaps it is the first pure relationship they've had since they became Christians. But marriage is not always the next logical step to take. Often God brings a person into your life *for the time being*, without a lifetime relationship in mind. You have to give him the freedom to do just that, without demanding more.

Going beyond the fundamental question of commitment to the Lord, consider how similar your goals and values are. Do you share a common mission in life, or is one person contemplating serving God overseas, while the other prefers to stay within twenty miles of home? Does one of you envision a normal suburban lifestyle with well-groomed children and average church attendance, while the other longs to invest time helping other people find Christ and grow in him? How similar are the price tags you each place on people and relationships as opposed to material possessions?

Love that will work in marriage includes a fusing of the minds; you feel the same about the important things. You can bare your soul to the other person and be understood and totally accepted. You have conflicts and quarrels, but you can iron out your differences without devastating each other's sense of worth.

As you evaluate each other's tastes, preferences, and interests, how much do you have in common? If a basketball player marries an opera lover, their relationship will not automatically be doomed, but they will have to learn to enjoy, or at least endure, each other's interests. Otherwise sparks will fly and tension will be present. How much better to be able to naturally enjoy some common interests together.

Personality

The last criterion for compatibility in relationships is explained in terms of *complementary* characteristics. We are attracted to people whose needs we can meet, and who in turn can meet some of our personality needs. Consciously or unconsciously, we enjoy the other's company because we experience a measure of completion in the presence of the other person.

Examples abound to illustrate this principle. George is a stable guy who thrives on being Sally's clear-headed, never-wavering partner. Sally in turn feels protected and secure with George. The person who is an impulsive, spur-of-the-moment planner is often attracted to someone who loves adventure. A talkative person often enjoys a relationship with someone who is a good listener.

Complementary characteristics are not to be confused with *contradictory* needs that are sometimes used as examples when we say, "Opposites attract." The fact that Ann is punctual while Jim is inherently late, or that Jeff is a spendthrift and Janet is a tightwad, means that both partners in both marriages will have to compromise for the sake of maintaining peace.

Although no two people are completely compatible, and God does use your differences to build character into each other's life, at some point you must face what those differences really are. Essentially, you must answer the question, How much do we have going for us and how much against us?

Whether or not you are seriously involved in a relationship with someone, take the opportunity to write down in as much detail as you want to, the character qualities and personality of the person you hope to marry someday. Pray about this list, and ask God to revise it as he desires. Then put it away somewhere. When you do begin to wonder if a particular relationship could develop into more than a friendship, compare the list to the person. Even though your needs and discernment may have changed with time, you will still find the list helpful. You can more quickly evaluate the relationship's potential.

When You Get Right Down to It

There is no simple, infallible formula to follow for choosing a marriage partner. If there were, we could just fill out a questionnaire and allow a computer to match us with the proper personality. To some degree, each of us will marry "by faith," but it need not be a faith that is blind or naive.

I'd like to challenge you to take on an interesting project. Ask some couples who are committed Christians with good marriages this question: How did you arrive at the conclusion that you should marry the person you did? In many cases, you will find a common element, as we have. We refer to it as "a holy fear."

Most people go through an intense period of seeking the Lord, arising as much from a fear of doing the wrong thing as a desire to make a truly wise choice within the will of God. We're encouraged when we see this taking place in a single person's life; we know the result will be not a flippant decision, but one for which he or she has truly waited on the Lord.

Perhaps some of the most useful advice that can be given is "*Wait and pray.*" "Show me your ways, O Lord, teach me your paths; guide me in your truth and teach me, for you are God my Savior, and my hope is in you all day long" (Psalm 25:4-5).

As you enter such a time of waiting on the Lord, don't neglect the opportunity to seek out the counsel of more mature Christians. The advice of parents, your pastor, a Bible study leader, and close friends is an important factor to weigh, because these people usually know you better in some ways than you know yourself. When Paula and I were contemplating marriage, the "green lights" we got from counsel were incredibly encouraging and reassuring.

Perhaps the entire process from dating casually to dating seriously to engagement could be underscored with this admonition: "Above all else, guard your heart, for it is the wellspring of life" (Proverbs 4:23). From the first date on, strong feelings must be ruled by clear thinking. Then when the appropriate time arrives, you can repeat the words *I do* with the firm assurance that you have made a wise choice.

Notes 1. James Peterson, as quoted in *Premarital Counseling*, by Norman Wright (Moody Press, 1977), page 22.

2. Maxine Hancock, "Commitment That Endures," *Family Life Today*, March 1981, page 20.

3. Robert K. Kelley, *Courtship, Marriage, and the Family* (Harcourt, Brace, Jovanovich, 1974), page 214.

4. Walter Trobisch, *I Married You* (Harper & Row Publishers, 1971), page 75.

5. Charles R. Swindoll, *Singleness* (Multnomah Press, 1981), page 13.

6. Ray Short, *Sex, Love, or Infatuation: How Can I Really Know?* (Augsburg Publishing House, 1978), page 17.

Questions for Personal Study and Application

1. What are your own definitions of infatuation and love?

2. What are the characteristics of real love as listed in 1 Corinthians 13:4–7?

3. God's giving of his Son is the perfect example of real love. Read John 3:16 and Romans 5:8, and describe love as God practices it.

4. Read 2 Samuel 13:1–19.
   a. What evidence is there that Amnon was infatuated with Tamar?
   b. What were the results of Amnon's infatuation? (You might also read verses twenty-three through thirty-eight.)

5. What are some right and wrong reasons to marry?

6. Describe in as much detail as you wish the kind of person you hope to marry someday. Concentrate on his or her character qualities. Begin to pray regularly about your desires.

7. Waiting on the Lord is essential in finding a mate. Look up Psalm 25:3, Isaiah 30:18 and 40:31, and Lamentations 3:25 and list the results of waiting and hoping in the Lord.

8. What personal application or commitment will result in your life, based on this study?

Scripture memory assignment: Matthew 6:33

Special project: Ask several couples why they decided they should get married.

Questions for Discussion

Question 1: When people in our culture speak of "love," do they most often mean infatuation or love?

Question 2: How can this passage be applied in evaluating a serious dating relationship?

Question 3: How does this kind of love compare with the love we should have for our spouse?

Question 4: What are some meanings a person might be communicating when he or she says, "I love you"? What are some ways in which that statement might be interpreted by the other person?

Question 5: Is it possible that two people may love each other in a mature way and yet decide that marriage is not right for them? Can you give an example?

Question 6: Do you believe there is only one right person for you to marry? Why or why not?

Question 7: How does Matthew 6:33 apply to looking for a mate or evaluating a serious dating relationship?

10

Growing into One

EVERYONE FANTASIZES his personal version of that life-changing event—becoming engaged. Amid candle-light and roses, speaking with a hushed voice, the moment of truth arrives: "Will you marry me?" Only four simple words, and yet life is never the same because of them.

Somewhere en route to the altar, Stacy and I bypassed the candles and roses. But you must understand that when Stacy makes up his mind to do something, he does it—right away. So after months of thinking and praying over the decision to marry, when he felt the time was right he wasted not a second, walked into the nearest phone booth, and called me halfway across the country.

Can you imagine being awakened from a dead sleep to address such a question? Groggy and incoherent as I was, that was one time I was at no loss for words. I've never been more sure of any decision in my life than the one to marry Stacy.

For others, the circumstances vary, the question may be couched in different words, and the answer may be less confident; each situation is as unique as the two individuals taking part. Becoming engaged is the first step in the joining of two lives, the blending of two personalities, the potential of many generations to come. So allow time before the point of engagement to make sure that each of you is mature enough to take on the responsibilities of a more intimate relationship. The engagement period is no time to grow up. Somehow once the ring is on her finger, life seems to be in limbo until you are pronounced "husband and wife."

Once you're engaged, you must allow enough time between the engagement and the wedding to make adequate preparations to spend the rest of your lifetime under the same roof. There are a myriad of things to think through and talk over. Some people mistakenly assume that once they are finally engaged to the person they believe to be the right one, the work is over. The truth is, planning for a lifetime together has just begun.

Preparing for a Lifetime Together

Engagement, for most couples, is a classic example of "the tyranny of the urgent" (the idea that we are so tyrannized and controlled by the urgent things of life that we have little time left for the really important things). Somehow the wedding arrangements will be taken care of—they always are. You have before you a much larger, though sometimes unrecognized task—that of preparing for a lifetime of interdependence and a meshing of two personalities.

Build a Strong Foundation

There's no substitute for premarital counseling. You need at least three sessions with someone who is personally interested in you, preferably the pastor who will marry you. Good premarital counseling can start you off on the right foot and alert you to patterns in your relationship that may already need to be changed. It's so much easier to help a couple do things right at the beginning than to help them *undo* a tangled relationship ten years later.

This is the time to develop your convictions together. There are so many things to talk about: budgets, birth control, an expanded version of your life goals, whether or not the wife should work and for how long, your relationship to your in-laws. The list goes on and on. The more you talk now, the fewer surprises you'll have on the other side of the altar.

To what degree should you discuss your past with your future partner? Many people have agonized over this question. Generally speaking, you need to discuss anything from your past that might have an effect on your future relationship together. Drug problems, abortion, a previous marriage, psychiatric disturbances, depression, and financial debts are some of the most common experiences that couples are forced to talk through.

You don't have to share every last detail. But if you face these issues before marriage, you invite a spirit of freedom, acceptance, and forgiveness that deepens your love. If the truth comes to light after marriage, it could poison your relationship with distrust and anger.

On the other side of the coin, there are some things you had best keep to yourself: "Initially I had reservations about marrying you because you aren't as pretty (or handsome) as I would have liked." "The people in your family are not my kind of people." When it comes to appearance and heritage, accept what you see, applaud the positive, and keep any other comments to a minimum.

This is the time to take another close, hard look at each other and answer this question: If he (or she) never changes, will I be happy with him? When each of you came to Christ, you in effect said, "Lord, take me just as I am." Unless you can come into marriage with that same attitude, you'd better rethink the whole proposition. Don't marry a person you are not willing to adjust to.

Now is the time to lay the foundation for good habits that will provide the "preventative maintenance" for your marriage relationship. From the time we were engaged, Stacy and I singled out one night a week as our "date night." We would go out for dinner or dessert, just to talk. It's amazing how much you can learn about someone over a two-hour cup of coffee with no distractions. Though it sounds so simple and obvious, over the last ten years this habit has helped us keep close to the pulse of each other's life more than any other single factor. And it all began during our engagement.

Another practice we instituted at that point was faithfully asking each other's forgiveness. To anyone who overheard us, it might have sounded ridiculous: "I'm sorry I forgot to pick up those cinnamon rolls you asked for.

Would you forgive me?" Little things, big things, any-thing—we were determined to keep short accounts with each other. Recently we noticed that we were letting friction build up, and that when we did air our disagreements we were stopping short of using that cleansing phrase, "I'm sorry. Would you forgive me?" We agreed anew to return to that habit of keeping the slate clean as faithfully as we did before.

This is the time to intensify the lifelong art of studying your partner. What are her greatest needs? What do his moods revolve around? How can we bring our conflicts to a point of mutual resolution? Dr. Howard Hendricks says, "If a young man can come into marriage with his paramount passion in life to completely satisfy his wife, and if the girl can come into marriage with her sole, exclusive purpose the satisfaction of her husband, and both are sold out to satisfying Jesus Christ, then you have the ingredients for an ideal Christian marriage."[1]

For a man to meet the deeper needs of his wife, he must love her as Christ loved the church in laying down his life for her (Ephesians 5:25). This is far more than remembering her birthday and buying Valentine candy. She has a strong need for *security* and a feeling of *worth and value*. She needs to know that her husband is looking out for the family, that he's planning in a certain direction. The cure for a nagging wife is a husband who becomes a planner and communicator.

Even in this day and age, when a woman's value is so often measured by her standing in the marketplace, there is no substitute for being valued in the eyes of her husband. These are words that a woman longs to hear: "Tell me what you think about that idea, honey." "I really need your opinion of this situation." Most women value social inter-course (communication) as intensely as their husbands value sexual intercourse, and woe to the marriage that does not thrive on both.

On the other hand, Scripture indicates that a man's greatest need is that of *respect*. "Wives, submit to your own husbands as to the Lord. . . . The wife must respect her hus-band" (Ephesians 5:22 and 33). He needs to feel that his wife is supporting him and willing to follow his leadership. A man might say, "Honey, I just need to feel the encour-agement that you are on my team, that you're for me."

The needs of your partner may manifest themselves in different ways over the years, even though they spring from the same roots. Engagement is the time to start developing your skill at assessing those needs.

Instead of losing sleep over the tuxedos, I'm so thank-ful that Stacy used the period of our engagement to bear down in prayer for our future together. God did so faith-fully answer these requests (and continues to do so) that perhaps they merit your consideration.

1. individually, that we might seek God's face first (Matthew 6:33)
2. that our lives and our marriage would reflect the true Light (Christ) in such a way that our family and friends could bear witness to it (Matthew 5:16)
3. that God would lead me as I direct the paths of our lives (Psalm 32:8)
4. that God would make me sensitive to Paula, put-ting her needs before mine (Ephesians 5:28–29)
5. that God would teach me to read her moods, feelings, likes and dislikes

6. that our wedding would glorify the Lord and uplift him

7. that our children would grow to be men and women of God (Psalm 103:17-18)

8. that we would experience the range of each other's emotional make-up—anger, sorrow, boredom, and so on—before marriage

9. that Paula would daily see my love for her and that we would enjoy life together (Ecclesiastes 9:9)

Resolve Your Past Conflicts

If you admitted to a marriage counselor that you were $5,000 in debt, he'd probably advise you to get a good job, take care of your debts, and then consider marriage. It's just too much strain on a relationship to start out in the hole financially.

In the same way, emotional debts and broken relationships can become a strain on your marriage. Friction and conflict in especially intimate relationships such as with your mother or father, or your sister or brother, must be resolved, or in a very real sense you can never leave home. Every time your wife makes a remark that sounds like your mother, anger will boil within you. Scripture says it so well: "See to it that no one misses the grace of God and that no bitter root grows up to cause trouble and defile many" (Hebrews 12:15).

One friend related an interesting story about how she resolved her relationship with her brother before her marriage. "I realized there was an unspoken tension between us," she said, "mostly due to the overbearing, selfish way I treated him as my younger brother. I went to him and admitted my failures, asked his forgiveness, and started off on a new footing with him. I really believe that if I had not taken that step, the past would have dominated my future relationship with him and the harmony between our two families."

Now is the time to deal with all your past debts, financial and otherwise. "If it is possible, as far as it depends on you, live at peace with everyone" (Romans 12:18).

You Are, But Then Again You Aren't

There is no time in your life quite like that of being an engaged couple. You aren't quite single any more, and goodness knows, you aren't married. Most of the time you are discussing life as it's going to be, not life as it is now. You've waited with such anticipation to ask or answer the question, Will you marry me? Why, then, isn't engagement a state of perpetual ecstasy?

You will be comforted to know that for most people, engagement is a peculiar time of transition accompanied by predictable seasonal storms. For one thing, you are probably more tired than you realize. You may be weary of planning a wedding, tired of bouncing ideas back and forth between two sets of parents, and exhausted from finishing school or details at work. Many couples make the unfortunate mistake of beginning marriage so tired and exhausted that after the wedding they collapse on some remote beach.

While it is the event of a lifetime, the object of a wedding is to become husband and wife, not stage the social event of the year. Many people (women in particular) fall prey to "weddingitis"; that is, they get so absorbed in finding the proper lace for the bridesmaids' dresses that they forget the focus is a *relationship*, not a one-day event.

Another seasonal storm to anticipate is fear. "What if she eats green onions in bed?" "What if he chews tobacco in church?" "Suppose we're pressured to eat Sunday dinner every week at her mother's house?" And on and on.

Engagement has tremendous ups and downs. In your effort to be honest and transparent, don't make the mistake of sharing every negative emotion with your future spouse, unless you begin to have *serious* doubts about your prospective marriage. Just knowing that everyone goes through some of this should help. After all, you're making the second biggest decision of your life.

You've Waited This Long

Perhaps the greatest tension most couples experience is in the physical arena. If you've waited this long to experience physical oneness, you can wait a few more months. It's terribly important that you *do* wait.

For one thing, you have to face the fact that fifty percent of the couples who say, "Let's get married" don't make it to the altar. Engagement is a time when either party can say, "I just don't think this is going to work." You don't need sex to complicate the situation.

Secondly, you'll be far ahead in the challenge of sexual adjustment if you enter marriage free from guilt. One pastor we know asks each couple he marries to write out a contract together of the limits they will set in physical involvement during their engagement period. Then he says, "Mark it down that I am personally going to ask you on the day that I marry you if you kept this agreement. I want you to be able to look your children straight in the eye when you tell them *why* they must be home by midnight."

Maybe you won't go as far as signing a piece of paper, but you must discuss the limits of your involvement. The temptation to proceed on to the point of no return is incredible.

The Right Person at the Right Time

There's more to getting married than finding the right person to marry. To ensure the smoothest transition from single to married life, you will want to marry the right person at the right time. What is the best length for an engagement period? Perhaps you've known couples who were engaged three weeks, and others, three years. Today they're happily married.

Generally speaking, the engagement period needs to be long enough to confirm or negate your decision to marry, and short enough to keep from losing your mind. William Coleman aptly states, "The engagement period is *not* the best time to get to know each other. Date each other for one, two, three, ten years if you want. But once you say, 'We are going to get married,' do not pass Go and do not collect $200. Take the shortest route to the altar and get married. If you are not prepared to get married for a year or more, don't get engaged."[2]

Obviously there are extenuating circumstances. Weddings must be paid for; you'd like your families to be well and present; it would be wise to have a job. But the principle remains: If you have to wait much longer than a year, then wait to get engaged.

As you consider the question, When should we get

married? be careful how many *new* things you will taking on at one time. Three days after we got married, we moved halfway across the country to a town new to both of us, where we knew no one, to a new job, and to a new relationship—ours.

I am one of those rare females who cries about twice a year, for five minutes each time, over some silly movie or situation when everyone else laughed. During the first six months of our married life, I cried about once a week. And since I was extremely happy with Stacy, we were both at a loss to diagnose the malady. Finally, we reached the verdict: too many new things at once. Avoid such circumstances if there is any way possible.

Anticipate and plan your wedding together as much as possible, especially the ceremony. Enjoy the first fruits of working together on a common project. But if tensions mount and the groom-to-be finds himself debating with his future sister-in-law the merits of stainless steel over sterling silver, then reconsider his role in the less important details. Since the bride's family usually pays for these affairs, follow the golden rule: The man with the gold, rules.

Christian Marriage—A Lifetime Commitment

A friend of ours who married at a very young age once told me that on her honeymoon she began to feel she'd made a terrible mistake. She called her father in tears and told him she wanted to come home and forget the whole affair. "Honey," he said, "those vows you made the other day, you made before God. And he is well able to help you work them out. You stay right where you are." She did, and twenty-five years later she's very glad she did.

Now most of you will never reach such an extremity, especially on your honeymoon. But it's good to remember that the vows you take before friends and family, you also repeat before the living God. Those words cannot be spoken lightly. C. S. Lewis said we sign a contract when we marry because we realize that there will be periods of conflict, boredom, and monotony. Marriage before God is one room in which there is no exit except the door marked "death."

Marriage can take you to some of the greatest heights you've ever known. Then again, there are days when you wonder how two such different people ever got together. I love to reread a statement that Dick Halverson made about his own marriage.

> The first element is commitment, despite the differences. My wife and I are married for life. I have an arrangement with Doris that God witnessed as an unconditional covenant for life. No matter how difficult it is to live together, we're going to stay married. Every struggle we have that could be used as an excuse to separate or divorce is the very material God wants us to use to create intimacy in our marriage. We can't get it any other way; it comes by hammer and heat. Good marriages are always forged.[3]

After resolving a clashing disagreement, Stacy reminded me, "Honey, you know that I'm just a sinner, shot through and through." Thereupon I nicknamed him the "big sinner" and me the "little sinner" (no reference to the quantity of sin intended). Even now we occasionally refer to each other by our nicknames (especially during times of stress) because those names remind us that we're just two sinners married to each other.

Marriage is a private school in which you can develop the love that says, "I accept you even if I have to listen to the same corny jokes for the next fifty years." As two people learn the real meaning of love, hashing through the daily realities of life together, they emerge better equipped to love others outside of their classroom.

Charlie Shedd is well-known for many things, not the least of which are his illustrations about marriage. He likens the merging of two people into one entity to two streams that converge at one point with great force, even considerable spray and foam. But eventually, from their union a river emerges, luxuriously broad and deep.

Marriage is an adventure that begins at an altar and ends at a graveside. In between there will be laughter and tears, anger and ecstasy. As the Lord brought you together, he will see you through. May you ever turn back to him, who was and who is and who is to come, for "unless the Lord builds the house, its builders labor in vain" (Psalm 127:1).

Notes   1. Howard Hendricks, "Yardsticks of Love."

2. William L. Coleman, *Engaged* (Tyndale House Publishers, 1980), page 23.

3. "Planting Seeds and Watching Them Grow," an interview with Dr. Richard C. Halverson, *Leadership*, Fall 1980, page 19.

Questions for Personal Study and Application

1. Do you believe that marriage has some guarantees; for example, that you will never have to make another decision by yourself? If so, what are these guarantees?

2. Is it always a good idea to begin talking about marriage before the guy proposes? Why or why not?

3. What do you believe are the purposes of engagement?

4. What are some topics and questions an engaged couple should talk about?

5. What are some ways in which Satan might attempt to damage or destroy a strong Christian relationship between an engaged couple?

6. What should be true about a couple's shared devotional life before they get married?

7. While they were engaged, the authors began two important practices to strengthen their marriage. What did they do? What are some things you think might be important habits to form as a couple?

8. To what degree do you "marry" your in-laws? Should your attitude and relationship with them be a consideration in getting married?

Scripture memory assignment: Psalm 127:1

Special project: List those things you would like to be true of your life as a single person before you get married.

Questions for Discussion

Question 2: Are there any topics about which a difference of opinion is important enough to indicate that a couple should not get married? If so, what do you think they are?

Question 3: How much time, in general, do you think it takes to plan the wedding and make other arrangements such as a place to live?

Question 4: How would you go about setting guidelines for your physical relationship?

Question 5: If an engaged couple disagree about some decisions concerning the wedding, how should they be handled?

Question 6: What are some requests you would include as you regularly prayed about your approaching marriage?

Question 7: What can you do to make engagement a joyful time, not just a busy time?

Question 8: How important is it to speak to the parents of the girl before you propose formally?

Bibliography

Clarkson, Margaret. *So You're Single!* Wheaton, Illinois: Harold Shaw Publishers, 1978.

Coleman, William L. *Engaged: When Love Takes Root.* Wheaton, Illinois: Tyndale House, 1980.

Collins, Gary R. *It's OK to Be Single.* Waco, Texas: Word Books, 1976,

DeSanto, Charles P. *Love and Sex Are Not Enough.* Scottsdale, Pennsylvania: Harold Press, 1977.

Fooshee, George and Marjean. *You Can Beat the Money Squeeze.* Old Tappan, New Jersey: Fleming H. Revell, 1980.

Friesen, Garry. *Decision Making and the Will of God.* Portland, Oregon: Multnomah Press, 1981.

Hartley, Fred. *Update*. Old Tappan, New Jersey: Fleming H. Revell, 1977.

Karssen, Gien. *Getting the Most Out of Being Single*. Colorado Springs, Colorado: NavPress, 1983.

Kirby, Scott. *Dating: Guidelines from the Bible*. Grand Rapids, Michigan: Baker Book House, 1979.

Mayhall, Jack and Carole. *Marriage Takes More Than Love*. Colorado Springs, Colorado: NavPress, 1978.

Petersen, J. Allan. *Before You Marry*. Wheaton, Illinois: Tyndale House, 1974.

Short, Ray E. *Sex, Love, or Infatuation: How Can I Really Know?* Minneapolis: Augsburg Publishing House, 1978.

Swindoll, Charles R. *Singleness*. Portland, Oregon: Multnomah Press, 1981.

Trobisch, Walter. *Love Yourself*. Downers Grove, Illinois: InterVarsity Press, 1979.

Wheat, Ed. *Love Life for Every Married Couple*. Grand Rapids, Michigan: Zondervan Publishing House, 1980.

White, John. *Eros Defiled: The Christian and Sexual Sin*. Downers Grove, Illinois: InterVarsity Press, 1977.

Wright, H. Norman. *Communication: Key to Your Marriage*. Ventura, California: Regal Books, 1974.

Wright, H. Norman, and Marvin Inmon. *A Guidebook to Dating, Waiting, and Choosing a Mate*. Eugene, Oregon: Harvest House, 1978.